Small Wonder

Small Wonder

How to Answer
Your Child's
Impossible Questions
About Life

Jean Grasso
Fitzpatrick

VIKING

VIKING
Published by the Penguin Group
Penguin Books USA Inc., 375 Hudson Street,
New York, New York 10014, U.S.A.
Penguin Books Ltd, 27 Wrights Lane, London W8 5TZ, England
Penguin Books Australia Ltd, 10 Alcorn Avenue,
Toronto, Ontario, Canada M4V 3B2
Penguin Books (N.Z.) Ltd, 182–190 Wairau Road, Auckland 10, New Zealand

Penguin Books Ltd, Registered Offices:
Harmondsworth, Middlesex, England

First published in 1994 by Viking Penguin,
a division of Penguin Books USA Inc.

1 3 5 7 9 10 8 6 4 2

Grateful acknowledgment is made for permission
to reprint the poem on page 183 from *Children's
Letters to God: The New Collection,* Stuart
Hample and Eric Marshall, editors.
Copyright 1991 by Stuart Hample and Eric
Marshall. Reprinted by permission of
Workman Publishing. All rights reserved.

ISBN 0-670-84691-0
CIP data available

Printed in the United States of America
Set in Minion
Designed by Vicki Hartman

To Robert Freeman
in memoriam
and for Vivienne,
Nicholas, and Amanda

Contents

Acknowledgments

Many thanks to my colleagues in the Hudson Group for their collective wisdom and good humor; to my agent, Heide Lange, for her unflagging enthusiasm and shared experiences of parenthood; and to Mindy Werner, my editor at Viking, for bringing her care, sensitivity, and clear thinking to the challenges of this project.

My years at the Maryknoll School of Theology helped me recognize the ways in which we all explore profound questions in the context of our social and cultural experience. And to my colleagues—students and faculty—at the Westchester Institute, I am grateful for many insights into the importance of questions and the centrality of meaning in everyday human problems.

I would like to thank all the parents who have attended my workshops; all the clergy and religious educators in various parts of the country who have generously shared their own questions, stories, and hospitality during the writing of this book; the children whose questions and struggles appear in these pages; friends and colleagues at the Foundation for Religion and Mental Health; and the people I accompany on the questioning path in my practice as a psychotherapist.

I thank my husband, Des, for asking more questions than any other grown-up I know, and my children, Laura and Matthew, whose challenges and eagerness keep me honest. And for my own questions and the courage to keep asking when answers seem most elusive, I offer thanks to the Source of all wonder.

Prologue

> The serious problems of life are never fully solved. If it
> should for once appear that they are, this is the sign
> that something has been lost.
>
> —Carl Jung

As parents today, we don't blush or stammer when we describe the mechanics of copulation, or when we tell our children about the microscopic union of sperm and egg. Other subjects are more challenging. "It's a lot easier for me to talk to my kids about sex," parents tell me, "than to answer questions about death or God."

Today we lack answers to questions our great-grandparents took for granted. Traditional ways of understanding love, death, money, and God seem to raise more questions than they resolve. Science and theology point toward complex, ambiguous explanations of the nature of life and the universe. As we reach midlife many of us are struggling, reexamining questions we haven't seriously considered in years, and discovering new ones. We know life's gray areas. We don't want to offer pat answers, or one-dimensional thinking, to the children we love.

After my book *Something More: Nurturing Your Child's Spiritual Growth*, was published, I started traveling around the country giving lectures and workshops on the shared spiritual journey of parents and children. At first, I was worried. Would parents complain that my advice was impractical? Would they demand more "handy tips" on children's spirituality? To my surprise, audiences seemed to appreciate my *not* offering shortcuts. They were eager to share and explore their own experiences, their own stories. Talking with parents of different cultural and religious backgrounds, I find we face similar struggles.

"You know, I'm beginning to realize that I can't really answer my kids' questions until I figure out what *I* think about things," mused one young father in Portland, Oregon. "Do you know if there's any such thing as 'theology therapy'?"

The man's question echoed in my mind for months afterward. It was a reminder that in a child's life difficult questions are not about an assortment of isolated topics, but represent aspects of something deeper and all-encompassing, something the theologian Paul Tillich referred to as "ultimate concern," the spiritual reality that underlies our existence from birth to death. Hands-on experiences and the element of fantasy, so much a part of the young child's spirituality which I had explored in *Something More*, give way, by school age, to questions about the origins and workings of the everyday world. At any age, reflecting on these questions deepens our awareness and enriches our being. It is a spiritual path that opens naturally in the context of family life, if we keep our eyes and ears open.

Having written about child-rearing for more than a dozen years, and with two inquisitive children of my own, I have long been intrigued by the ongoing connection between existential or spiritual awareness and the crises (ordinary and traumatic) of family life. I was eager to explore the questioning process in the context of the child's growth as a whole person, a small explorer seeking with considerable urgency to make sense of the world around him. And so I decided to write this book.

Most of the advice available for parents on children's questions is narrowly based on developmental theory, with apparently little recognition that questions are the stepping-stones along a child's spiritual path. They offer practical answers, yet rarely do they seek to help us meet our children's need to piece together their concrete experiences at home and school. Religious educators, on the other hand, too often dampen a child's propensity to wonder by presenting a particular tradition as the answer, rather than by inviting her to discover within that tradition sources of timeless wisdom and companionship on the journey.

As a parent, workshop leader, and therapist, I often remind myself that questions come up in the context of everyday life, and that when we stay right there—looking at our own experience, not reaching for "higher" truths—we grow. The approach you will find in these pages draws on my formal study of existential psychoanalysis—not exactly "theology therapy," but an approach to life's ordinary challenges and ambiguities that, drawing on the writings of Heidegger, Kierkegaard, and more recently Viktor Frankl,

Rollo May, Irvin Yalom, and others, suggests rich possibilities for deepening our individual experience of meaning. By understanding questions in the context of psychoanalytic theory and spiritual development, you can learn to recognize how clearly these questions connect with a child's deepest needs, wishes, and conflicts.

Like all mothers, I know that theories are helpful but never the whole story. Parenting manuals that offer formulaic answers don't leave us room to convey our own values, to connect questions with the ups and downs of our particular family, to share our own questions. Authentic responses to children's questions—to *all* questions—are born of *struggle*. For myself, and for the parents who shared their advice and dilemmas as I researched this book, engaging in real dialogue with kids demanded a willingness to grow. If we are to keep pace with our children's questioning, we parents need to be open to exploration, too. We need to bring our whole selves to the task. We need to draw on our own imaginative powers—to be comfortable with paradox, to rediscover the wisdom in the stories of our own families and traditions, to know and trust our own life experience and instincts, our wins and losses, our mistakes.

This book is incomplete without your participation. There are many ways to speak eloquently of love, or God, or death, but *your* responses will reflect all that you know of your child's circumstances, history, and temperament. Only you can help your child piece together his or her daily experiences, observations, worries, and talents. I hope you will discover that you can bring your soul into questioning dialogues, in the tradition of sages and storytellers of generations past, and face your child's questions with wisdom, courage, and love.

Small Wonder

·1·

Why Questions Matter

The true problems of living ... have no solution in the ordinary sense of the word. They demand of man not merely the employment of his reasoning powers but the commitment of his whole personality.
—E. F. Schumacher, *Small Is Beautiful*

Children ask extraordinary questions in the process of discovering the world, questions that reawaken us to the wonder of life—and remind us how little we adults understand. "How come you can say *damn* and we can't?" "Does God know the future?" "Why are bad people bad?" Often, especially when times are hard in our family or community, a child's innocent inquiries touch on our deepest fears, doubts, and sorrows. "No kidnappers live around

here, do they, Mom?" "Why were you and Daddy fighting?"
or "Why doesn't God feed the poor people?"

Healthy children are too alive, and too aware, to accept or
learn from easy answers. This book is for parents and caregivers who appreciate that. That human beings learn and
grow through questioning is ancient wisdom. Since the time
of Socrates, philosophers have understood that asking questions builds insight and imagination. At the Passover meal,
the youngest child asks the Four Questions. The psychiatrist
Robert Coles noted in his study of children's spirituality
that "The questions Tolstoy asked, and Gauguin in . . . his
great Tahiti triptych, completed just before he died ('Where
Do We Come From? What Are We? Where Are We going?'),
are the eternal questions children ask more intensely, unre-
mittingly, and subtly than we sometimes imagine."

I've heard many parents tell of the difficulty of answering
hard questions honestly without confusing or frightening
their kids. And yet most of us find the questions thought-
provoking, even exhilarating. We stumble and stammer, but
still we recognize our children's questions as welcome signs
of their natural curiosity, wonder, and creativity. Children
who have a healthy relationship with their parents naturally
trust that life has meaning: They are eager to explore it at
every opportunity. In asking a question a child shows her
trust in us and a conviction that, even though things go
wrong, the universe somehow makes sense. The way we listen, and the answers we offer, deliver a powerful message
about how much we value our children's point of view and
their ability to think for themselves.

If we fail to respond to our children's questions—if we
shrug them off, or deny the troublesome reality they point
to, like the adults did to the observant child in the tale of the

Emperor's new clothes—then we teach them not to trust their own perceptions. If children are to grow up to be whole people, capable of living responsibly and lovingly in the world, they need to learn early on that we *listen* to them, that we trust *their* logic, that we are willing to help them explore their *own* meaning. This is not a matter of teaching them to be "philosophical" or "deep"; *it is the essence of recognizing a child as the protagonist of his or her own life.*

Day after day I see the importance of this in many of the adults who come to me to talk over their frustrations and disappointments with partners, family, or career. Often the problems they bring are difficult, but far from intractable; the real difficulty is that they, like many people, have never learned to trust their own instincts. When our observations and questions are not listened to, we learn to accept the views of the adults around us. From our earliest days, we are taught *not to trust our own experience.* As a result, we lose our inner compass, drown out our inner voice. As I work with people who have suffered these losses and they begin to honor their own perceptions of things, they come to recognize that they are more powerful than they realized. They know the truth about their own lives. They can work to solve their own problems.

By attending to a child's questions, we nurture her whole self. Far from being detours into esoteric inquiry, questions can lead us into the center of life. "How often have I heard a patient exclaim: 'If only I knew that my life had some meaning and purpose, then there would be no silly story about my nerves!' " wrote Carl Jung, who observed that the search for meaning draws not only on our reasoning powers, but on our creativity and capacity for love. This is an age when so many children seem to grow up lacking meaning and purpose—and end up filling the void with drinking, drugs, and sex, or falling into apathy or suicidal depression—and children need help and support as they grapple with the questions of meaning they face at even the tenderest ages. If children's explorations are not encouraged, if their wondering is not affirmed, and if they do not learn to probe, to use their critical faculties, they passively take in the images and adopt the empty values of their most persuasive peers, Madison Avenue, and television.

In *Man's Search for Meaning*, the psychiatrist Viktor Frankl, a survivor of the Nazi death camps, explored the connection between a person's sense of meaning and his ability to "say yes to life," to keep faith in the future in the face of uncertainty and even tragedy. Frankl believed that neither sexuality nor the desire for power but a "will to meaning" was humanity's basic motivational force. He was fond of quoting Nietzsche: "He who has a *why* to live can bear with almost any *how*."

Today's children face so many choices in life, more than our grandparents ever dreamed. And yet every day's paper brings news of hunger and homelessness, of the AIDS epidemic, of ethnic warfare, of ecological devastation. Our children are growing up, much more than our generation did, acutely aware of life's *limitations*. If we are so worried about giving our children bad answers that we have nothing at all to say, we fail to prepare them for the challenges of the decades to come. If we simply reassure them, we are cheating our children of the opportunity to learn, to grow, and to face the issues that trouble them.

For this reason, this book is not a collection of sanitized answers designed to reassure your child that there is really nothing to worry about. Children know better. Our children's future on this planet demands that they be much more than secure and "well-adjusted." Through questioning dialogue, we can help our children develop the creative thinking, moral imagination, and enduring hope they will need to find meaning and make a difference in their own lives and their world.

Questions and Your Family Life

In the midst of our busy lives, questioning dialogue sparks moments of authentic sharing that deepens family bonds. Our culture tends to value action more than talk, and home life often revolves around getting to and from a series of activities. Yet when we are busy driving to daycare or music lessons, or putting laundry in the dryer, and a child suddenly asks a question that leaves us wondering, "How did he come up with *that?*" it is important to remember that real talk is at the heart of every relationship. Long before children can even understand words, language itself creates a deep bond between parent and child.

The thirteenth-century historian Salimbene recorded that the German emperor Frederick II wanted to discover what would happen if children grew up without hearing words. Frederick told foster mothers and nurses to feed, bathe, and wash children but not to speak to them. He thought he would discover whether the infants would spontaneously speak Hebrew, Greek, or Latin, or the language of their parents. "But he laboured in vain because the children all died," Salimbene wrote. "For they could not live without the petting and joyful faces and loving words of their foster mothers." Making real conversation a priority—honoring its importance in the midst of your family's hectic schedule of work, school, and activities—fulfills your child's most urgent need.

Think of dialogues with your child as your part in the oral tradition. As your child puzzles over the world, and you respond with your whole self, together you create a dialogue that is like shared storytelling. Listening to children wonder about where they come from, what romantic love feels like, and who God is, gives parents an opportunity for fresh understanding of old ways. It is a dance of sorts. "Babies control and bring up their families as much as they are controlled by them," wrote Erik Erikson in *Childhood and Society.*

When your child asks questions, he is not only asking for information about the events around him; like the story of Adam in the garden, who learned to relate to other living creatures by naming them, the child who puts his wonder into words is deepening the connections between himself and his world. He is like the lover who wants to know everything about the beloved, and in doing so loves her more. ("Daddy, do you have hormones?" one six-year-old asked.) Like a toddler—who endlessly experiments with lights that switch on and off, cups that can be filled and emptied, and loved ones who can be approached and run away from—the child asking questions is grappling with profound issues through everyday exploration. Day by day the child pieces together fragments of reality as though they were collage materials, making connections that surprise and delight— and bewilder—adults. ("Why did God let the dinosaurs die?" asked one four-year-old.) The process is creative and above all, *playful.*

When we find ourselves struggling for answers that are

both reasonable and truthful, it is encouraging to keep in mind that *a child is rarely seeking—and nearly never satisfied with—a purely rational response to a question.* Children don't hear our answers and analyze them logically one by one (although they do have a knack for picking up on our inconsistencies!). They don't need to know all the details, or hear about things our instincts tell us are meant for adult ears. Instead, children need answers that make sense to them in the context of life as they know it. Their understandings of the mysterious and important aspects of the adult world—received through close relationships and everyday events—become part of who they *are*, of their developing characters, their young bodies, their growing selves.

The most memorable lesson about questions is a very old one. It is found in the answer to the most ancient question written down in our culture: I have in mind the first question spoken by a human being in the Bible, the moment when Cain asks God, "Am I my brother's keeper?"

The God of Genesis offers no abstract answer, no philosophical speculation. "What have you done?" God demands sorrowfully. "Your brother's blood calls to me from the ground." God in this story speaks with passion for life on this earth, of human *action*, and of its tragic consequences.

Passion and groundedness in the world around us: These are the essential qualities that loving caregivers bring to dialogues with children. They are the stuff not of philosophical speculation, but of *story.* Rather than reaching for clever replies, we are more helpful when we talk about familiar people and places and connect questions with the daily events of our shared lives. We can trust that our *feelings* about the questions—our sadness, our pain, our perplexity—are not liabilities but signs of caring. We can stop berating ourselves about the things we don't know. What our children need most is not philosophizing, but our willingness to reflect on our own everyday experience and to connect with our inner wisdom.

How to Use This Book

In the pages that follow, you will learn how to respond to your child's difficult questions and explore them in the context of everyday family life. Every chapter is devoted to a different topic—love, ethics, money, death, the cosmos, and God. Each one consists of a four-part approach: developmental background information, sample questions and answers, projects for parents and kids to do together, and exercises for parents.

The developmental information helps you connect your child's questions to his or her social, cognitive, emotional, and spiritual growth. I've drawn from child development research, psychoanalytic theory (particularly from existential analysis and the work of Erik Erikson, who taught us so much about the way our inner lives unfold in the context of the world around us), as well as from the work of theorists of moral growth and faith development, who focus on the evolution of world-views in children and adults. You'll find advice on how to use words your child can understand, and how to encourage her to work toward her own answers at different ages.

The sample questions and answers are based on conversations with parents who have attended my workshops and lectures, and on a wide range of sources, ancient and modern, sacred and secular. They are grouped according to age; you will learn the pivotal questions children ask at different stages, how to listen for the unspoken issues behind a child's questions, and how the same question needs to be approached in different ways at different stages.

When your child's question catches you by surprise, or when he asks about a painful problem, I hope you will find it reassuring to know you can find an answer—or several answers—close at hand. (You can also hear how other parents have replied to questions your child is likely to ask, today or next year or several years from now.) You will discover how to avoid setting up an opposition between scientific knowledge and religious tradition. You will learn how to help your child evaluate ideas she has heard from peers or the media. You will find out how to say "I don't know" without closing off discussion and growth.

Because the answers are based on the experiences of parents of diverse backgrounds and traditions, as well as on my own beliefs about what's healthy for kids, you are likely to agree with many of them but disagree strongly with others. I hope that you will find them thought-provoking. Depending on your child's age, the occasion, and your own instincts, you may wish to use only the first sentence or two of a particular answer. As often as possible, I've included suggestions on how to personalize the sample answers by drawing on your own experience, including the people and places that are a familiar part of your family life and that will be the most meaningful to your child. You will find advice on what *not* to say. Finally, when questions are disturbing, you will learn how to recognize when your child may benefit from professional help.

In "Exploring Together" you will find simple activities to nurture your child's inquiring mind. When you notice that she is particularly interested in a certain topic, these projects will give her a chance to dig deeper and turn your home into a place where curiosity and wonder are welcome. Each time you and your child try one of these activities, you help her questions open a path to a shared journey.

Finally, "The Parent's Path" contains exercises and questions to help you bring your own life experience to dialogues with your child. By reflecting on your thoughts and feelings about specific topics and questions, as well as the events in your life that have influenced your attitudes, you will learn how much you have to offer. Like parents of generations past, you will begin to enrich your responses by sharing stories—family lore, community history, and sacred stories. And if your life is so busy that you haven't spent much time wondering about things in recent years, these exercises will help you rediscover questioning for yourself, and appreciate that your child's efforts at making sense of things is deeply rooted in everyday life.

As you grow more confident and less anxious, I hope you'll find this book helps you to *enjoy* these dialogues. Together you and your child are learning, as the poet Rainer Maria Rilke wrote in a memorable letter to a young friend, to "*live* the questions now. Perhaps you will one day live into the answer." And in the months and years ahead I hope that you may come to discern in your child's difficult questions the promptings of the spirit.

• 2 •

The Art
of Listening
to a Child

Basic words, wrote Martin Buber, are spoken with one's being. Our children's questions, spoken simply and from the heart, are basic words. For this reason, learning to really *listen* to a child's questions is one of the most important things we parents do. "God gave man two ears, but only one mouth," wrote Epictetus the Stoic two thousand years ago, "that he might hear twice as much as he speaks."

When a child asks a puzzling question, we can get so caught up in finding an answer that we neglect to appreciate the value of our *attentiveness.* We grope for a meaningful response, only to discover our child has tuned us out or abruptly changed the subject.

Listening as Loving
Many people never experience the powerful healing effect of being truly attended to by another human being. And yet to know we are listened to, that we can speak and be *heard,*

is essential to our humanity. The word *absurd* comes from the Latin *surdus,* "deaf or mute"; if we cannot hear or be heard, life has no meaning. Helen Keller wrote that, for her, deafness was a deeper, more complex problem than blindness because it cut her off from "the most vital stimulus—the sound of the voice that brings language, sets thoughts astir and keeps us in the intellectual company of man." Active, involved listening forges a parent's bond with a child. It reassures the child that he can express himself and that he *matters* to the people who love him.

As a child explores the world and tries to understand it, our role as listeners is the most powerful tool we have to help her link her inner world of play and the events and realities around her. The child's sense of self from infancy is dependent on her ability to make connections between her inner and outer worlds.

A child in the process of making these connections does not have the sophistication to verbalize them, of course, but history has left us an eloquent testimony in the words of Helen Keller, who wrote of the first time she understood the link between language and the world around her, on a walk outdoors with her teacher. "We walked down the path to the wellhouse, attracted by the fragrance of the honeysuckle with which it was covered. Someone was drawing water and my teacher placed my hand under the spout." At that moment, young Helen's teacher helped her grasp the connection between language and physical reality. "As the cool stream gushed over one hand she spelled into the other the word *water,* first slowly, then rapidly. I stood still, my whole attention fixed upon the motions of her fingers. Suddenly I felt a misty consciousness as of something forgotten—a thrill of returning thought; and somehow the mystery of language was revealed to me. I knew then that 'w-a-t-e-r' meant the wonderful cool something that was flowing over my hand. That living word awakened my soul."

As the child moves toward independence, parents' willingness to listen is an essential support. A child needs someone to respond to his observations, to help him interpret the puzzling realities he is beginning to notice. He needs to think out loud. As adults, many of us have had the experience of needing to talk about something in order to understand or grasp a reality. We may need to go over an event repeatedly—we relive the joy of a birth by reciting every detail of the length of time between contractions to the cutting of the umbilical cord. We try to grasp the fear and sorrow of a terminal illness by describing every symptom and every treatment. *We make sense of things by talking about them, and this is a process that starts in early childhood.*

Listening Presence

Many of the people I meet seem to imagine that if only they were different, they would be much better parents. If only they had time to read the newspaper from cover to cover, if only they had endless patience to deal with questions at the "arsenic hour" before dinner, if only they had enough religious faith to offer airtight explanations of life's problems, then they could offer neutral, enlightened answers to their children's questions.

What our children really need, though, is not a neutral adviser but a *conscious, caring* one. They need our full humanity, our genuine *presence.* They need us to be the down-to-earth people we really are, with the capacity to love, to hate, to be affectionate, to get angry, to appreciate their joyous innocence, to be wary of the ways of the world. They need our help sorting out their experience, which is something we can do best if we are willing to reflect on our own experiences—not necessarily to share the details with them, of course, but to convey the truths we are learning from our own lives. Our children need *us* to listen to them, and not some other, more "objective" person, because we care so passionately about *them*. Our answers reflect our understanding of our particular child and our hopes and dreams for her future. They are intimately connected to the whole parent-child relationship. As D. W. Winnicott observed in an essay on moral growth, "there is *more to be gained from love than from education.*"

Just as trying to be neutral prevents us from being fully present to our children, so does being prisoners of our own anxieties and ambivalence. To be fully present is not to be free of conflict, but it is to be *aware*. When a particular question often makes us anxious, or when we notice ourselves changing the subject, that is usually a sign that we need to look inward. The question is probably stirring up something deep in ourselves, and in order to listen effectively to the child's question we need to attend to our own feelings about it. The more I understand how I have sought to come to terms with love, death, the cosmos, and God in my own life, and the more familiar I am with my own personal demons, the more attentively I can listen to another person's thoughts on these topics. The better I know my own life experience, my own loss of innocence, and the values that sustain me, the freer I am to respond spontaneously in the moment.

Tell your own truth. Speak from your experience. If someone we love is dying and a child asks, "Will he go to heaven?" we're far better off giving an answer we believe in than temporarily borrowing a religious belief in which we have little conviction. If a child asks a question about sex, we're likely to stammer and stutter if the things we want to tell her are difficult to reconcile with our own life experience or beliefs. To be truly present is to be *honest,* which doesn't mean telling a child things she is not ready for or things that have more to do with our own questions than with hers. We should also be careful not to tell her things that ring hollow in our own ears. Paradoxically, *listening* to our child's fear, anger, bewilderment, and sadness in the face of loss is far more comforting than offering pat answers. Our humble attention is a way of sharing sacred presence.

A Three-Step Approach

You're home from work, you're fixing dinner while your child does his homework at the kitchen table, and the telephone rings every ten minutes or so with news from the soccer coach, Scout leader, or class parent. Out of the blue your child asks, "What's child abuse?" Take a deep breath. If you launch into a long-winded explanation before you've really heard what's bothering your child, he is likely to repeat the question several more times—or tune you out. Instead, focus on *listening.*

Step One: Show empathy. Depending on your child's age, ask yourself, "Why is he coming up with this question?" When faced with what sounds like an imponderable query of cosmic dimensions, encourage him to speak in concrete terms about a specific situation.

Keep in mind that this does *not* mean he is eager to expound on all his thoughts and feelings. He may only wish to say a single sentence, such as, "I saw a baby that was beaten on the TV news. A man did it." Rather than ask for factual details, such as, "Was the man the baby's father?" or "Did the baby die?" focus on describing the way your child might have reacted emotionally:

"It must have been very scary."

"That man did a terrible thing."

"What an awful thing, to hit a little baby."

By empathizing with your child, you are validating his perception. Use simple, direct language.

Try to focus on the situation or question itself. You might overwhelm your child if you make pointed remarks such as, "You must be afraid someone will hit you [or your baby cousin] that way." Although it is often possible—and important—to talk about the child's own fears, since children rarely experience anything impersonally, it is wise to proceed slowly or your child may decide to stop talking altogether. With a preteen or adolescent, let him talk. By wondering out loud he comes to understand what he thinks.

With a child of any age, but particularly an adolescent, notice body language. He may say, "I don't care," or "It's no big deal," but if his eyes are downcast, he's slumped, and he looks sad, his feelings may be different from his words. He will respond if you avoid plunging in with a guess about how he really feels and simply express your concern in a low-key way: "You know, I'm worried about you lately. You've been looking a little down."

Sometimes sharing your own feelings on the subject (*not* "When I was your age," though) can help him put his into words.

A young child who asks about death or fatal illness, for example, is seeking reassurance, not a medical history or metaphysical "explanation." One day my daughter came home from kindergarten and said, "A kid told me his two-year-old cousin died of cancer."

"Oh, I'm sorry. How awful," I said.

"I think he should have worn suntan lotion," she said matter-of-factly.

"Suntan lotion only helps stop *skin* cancer," I told her. "This child could have had a different kind of cancer."

"What kind?"

"Oh, blood cancer," I said. "Or bone cancer."

She didn't reply, but later that day she suddenly asked, "How do you get blood cancer or bone cancer?"

"I don't know," I said. "We can read about it. It doesn't happen to children very often." I waited, and when she didn't respond right away, I added, "When it does, it's very sad."

"Yeah," she said quietly. She was silent for a few minutes.

"A kid at school told me his two-year-old cousin died of cancer," she said again, slowly. "He didn't say if it was bone cancer or blood cancer."

I've no doubt that this sad story will come up again as my daughter struggles to grasp the reality of a child's death, long before she is cognitively ready to "understand" what cancer is. As a mother, I find talking about the death of a child painful beyond words, yet only by opening up to my own fear can I empathize with my daughter's.

Step Two: Help the child connect the question with personal experience. Helping a child struggle toward meaningful responses to her own questions rather than handing her our own is in keeping with the original meaning of the word *education*: "to draw out." Happily, even if we lack what we consider adequate answers we can be very helpful by encouraging the child to take one small step.

A white second-grader, whose parents had enrolled him in a multiracial school so that he would have the opportunity to meet all kinds of children, stepped off the school bus one afternoon with a scowl. "How come the black kids play so rough on the playground?" he asked, and his mother gasped.

This particular little boy, as it turned out, had been kicked in the groin during an informal soccer game. His mother began by showing empathy; she resisted the well-meaning temptation to scold ("I don't ever want to hear you say anything like that again!") and instead let him express his pain and anger.

When the child was ready to talk calmly, it was time to teach him the difference between *personal experience* and *stereotyping*. "*Those* black children played roughly, but not *all* black children do," she said, and reminded her son of some happier experiences. "You know some black children in your class who don't play roughly, don't you?"

Step Three: Follow up. If a question recurs, it may be time to dig deeper, by sharing appropriate books or helping your child get involved in a related activity (see the "Exploring Together" sections in each chapter). If your child seems obsessed with money, for example, be sure she has an allowance large enough that it lets her experiment with saving, spending, making charitable contributions, and even investing (if only in baseball cards). If your child talks in racial stereotypes, consider how you can broaden his horizons. One mother, realizing her child was speaking from limited life experience in a homogeneous community and school system, decided to enroll him in a multicultural YMCA crafts program in a neighboring town and decided to make an effort to expand the family's social circle to include a wider diversity of people. In these pages you will find resources and ideas from parents across the country who are exploring the questions you face with your child.

Create an atmosphere that says important subjects are discussed in your household by sharing some aspects of your own life with your children. Spend a Sunday afternoon looking through family albums, answering your child's questions about all the people and places she sees. Mention an interesting project you're working on at the office—or tell her (briefly) what a frustrating day you had today.

Children work on their problem-solving skills in many areas of life. Even minor exchanges teach her something about how much you respect her learning process. If she chooses to put on a plaid blouse and striped pants in the morning, do you tell her it looks awful, or let her explain why her clothes "match really well"? When he organizes his play figures on a shelf you'd planned for books and games, do you make him move them or listen to how he plans to organize his whole room? When he makes a mistake— spilling milk at the table, forgetting to let the dog out, leaving his homework on the kitchen table instead of bringing it to school—do you let him experience the consequences of his actions and help him devise a plan for doing better next time, or ridicule him by labeling him "irresponsible," "clumsy," or worse? By encouraging your child to think things through and make decisions for herself when possible, and being available as a resource and support when she needs it, you affirm her way of looking at things. You teach her to learn from her mistakes.

Shared Exploration

The minute you step onto your soapbox, have you noticed how your child gets engrossed in play or actually leaves the room? Children learn about the big questions of life through the details they struggle with. If we offer generalizations or noble sentiments, we fail utterly to connect with the mundane truths they encounter on the playground, in the classroom, and at home. Answers cannot be handed down as aphorisms.

Happily, your child has the tools and talents to learn to respond to her *own* questions with your help. She approaches age-old conundrums with fresh eyes and ears, and often with the same gusto with which she takes her first step, learns to write letters on a page, and rides her first two-wheeler. She makes startling connections between the story she heard at the library last week and the goslings in the park this morning. If she is not satisfied with your answer, you are likely to overhear her demanding a better one from her big brother or the babysitter.

Rather than offering a simplistic answer, you're better off saying, "I don't know." Then you can begin to explore together. You can read, visit a museum, ask a friend or neighbor who is more knowledgeable on that particular subject.

Make time for occasions when opportunities to talk might naturally come up. Bake an apple pie. Plant a garden together. Go for a hike. The things that are on a child's mind have a way of coming up at times like these. Once a day, even if you only have fifteen minutes, see if your child would like to do something simple; depending on her age and preferences, she might like to dance to the radio, sing a song, or show you a new Lego creation.

Make it a point to spend ten minutes a day listening to your child without planning ahead. When your child begins chattering and you catch yourself drifting off, don't. Instead, pull up a chair and listen. Pay attention to what she has to say. Be sure you do not criticize her, try to teach her anything, or correct her. Just be there.

Like the rest of us, children have different biological clocks. One child may be firing questions through your shower curtain every morning, while another begs you to stay one more minute at bedtime because he needs to tell you something. If you notice that your routine seems to regularly short-change a child when she is most eager to talk to you, try to rearrange your schedule. Set the alarm five minutes earlier in the morning, for example, or make bedtime five minutes earlier so that you have longer to chat before he sleeps.

No parent is available as often as a child would like, of course. "It seems as though every time I'm diapering the baby, Jason comes up with something he desperately needs to tell me!" said a mother in one of my workshops. When you feel guilty you're most likely to snap at your child about how busy you are, which of course only makes you feel worse in the long run. "That's a question I'd really like to talk about with you," you can say. "Let's sit down and talk about it later when I can pay attention better." If you habitually forget about the question later on, ask your child to bring it up again: "You know, I'm so busy I'm worried I'm going to forget about this question. I really *do* want to talk about it with you—will you remind me?"

Let Your Child Lead

Children have a way of recognizing when you're gearing up for a serious heart-to-heart talk. You can tell because they escape to their rooms, or run to get an apple from the refrigerator. Your child is more likely to feel comfortable discussing questions with you if you respect her need for space. If you're adding oil to the car and your child asks, "What does it feel like when you fall in love?" don't put down the funnel. Some of the best exchanges happen in the midst of everyday family activities—washing the dishes, walking the dog. Don't push it.

Children can tell the difference between a *response* to a question and an attempt to *pressure* them into "opening up" or seeing things from a parent's point of view. They need to experience their own worries, their own fear or wonder, without having an adult tell them how they must be feeling first. By doing so they build self-confidence.

There is a famous story of a university professor who went to visit a Zen master. The master began to pour tea into his guest's cup. He poured and poured until the teacup overflowed. The professor, who had been holding his tongue, finally burst out: "It is too full. No more will go in!"

"Like this cup," replied the Zen master, "you are full of your own opinions. How can I show you Zen unless you first empty your cup?"

If we fill a child with our own thoughts and opinions, and leave no room for his observations, then we leave no room for wonder. We need to cultivate the beginner's mind, the mind that is free of habit, ready to accept, to doubt, to see in a fresh way. It is the state of mind we all find delightful in a young child. One way to seek it is to focus on *listening*.

When your child shares an experience or a thought, don't jump in with a response right away. If she is young, try squatting down to talk at eye level. For a school-age child, it may be enough to say, "Mmm," to show you're paying attention. Don't interrupt her or assume you know what she's about to say. Remember, your primary task is *listening*. Approach her in the spirit of information-gathering. You're interested in what she has to say, but you can wait until she's ready to tell you in her own way.

Avoid launching into a response that begins, "When I was your age . . ." By staying with *her* story and her feelings rather than bringing in your own—which may be very different, even if your experience was the same—you affirm her self-esteem and show that you respect her way of looking at the world. (Reflecting *inwardly* on your childhood memories can help you connect emotionally with your child's experience, but your dialogues will mean more to your child if you let her thoughts and feelings take center stage.)

If your child asks a question that's obviously worrying her, don't try to reassure her by saying, "Don't worry. It's nothing." She needs to know that she can have negative feelings. Especially for young children, the *idea* or mental image of a frightening reality is just as scary as the reality itself. For this reason telling her "That won't *really* happen" isn't helpful. Instead, before you attempt to help her unravel the content of what she is asking about, show empathy: "What a scary book!"

Expect her to change the subject. When Goldilocks, my

daughter's goldfish, died after several days of drooping at the bottom of the tank, Laura (who was five at the time) looked in and said matter-of-factly, "Goldie's dead." That was all? I was stunned. I'd been bracing myself for wails and tears. Half an hour later Laura was busy at the kitchen table. "I'm making a book, Mom," she said. "It's called, 'The Life of Goldilocks, Laura's Pet.' After that I'm going to make a tombstone for her funeral. It's going to say, 'Here Lies Goldilocks, Laura's Pet, Three Week Survivor.'" She needed to talk about Goldie in her own time, and to learn to cope with the death in her own way.

Children have secrets. They need to keep them. If our responses to their questions sound like cross-examinations, we deny them the opportunity to grow as separate, strong people. If a child asks, "Why don't some people have homes to live in?" don't immediately rush in to speculate about her fears of becoming homeless. Let her tell you what she wants to. If she closes the door to her room for a while, respect her wishes.

Sometimes you may have a hard time figuring out what your child needs. *Ask* her: "Do you feel like hearing advice? I remember when something like this happened to me when I was a little girl; do you want to hear how I felt about it?" "Do you need a hug? Do you want to draw, or play with toys for a while?"

When Questions Are Warning Signs . . .

Look for *changes* in your child's behavior pattern to tell you when something is deeply troubling her.

- If a child who ordinarily explores feelings (through talking, art, or imaginative play) suddenly seems quiet and listless, she may be anxious or depressed.
- A big talker who seems awfully quiet lately may be worried about something he's not comfortable talking about.
- A well-behaved child who is "hyper" may have a heavy burden on her mind.
- A child who suddenly asks one question after another about death may be having difficulty coping with grief, or be depressed.

All children go through periods of being more or less eager to share their thoughts. As they grow, they increasingly need to air their questions with other trusted adults—teachers, counselors, clergy. But if you are uneasy with your child's questioning pattern, have a gut feeling that she is uncomfortably silent, or notice other changes in behavior that seem to indicate a problem (see pages 117–18), know your own limitations. For your child's well-being, it may be wise to seek professional help.

When You Don't Like What You Hear . . .

One of the quickest ways to cut short questioning dialogue with your child is to respond defensively. Sometimes a child hits a nerve. The question may be a minor one that points up our own insecurities—like the evening, after a day's work, when my eight-year-old, watching me arrange some store-bought brownies on a paper plate for a school function, smirked and asked, "Are you hoping everybody will think they're homemade?" Or a child may inquire about a painful situation ("Why do you and Daddy fight?"). It's not easy to offer a helpful response when you're feeling upset or annoyed. Sadly, if you do get indignant ("Don't you *dare* ask me something like that!" or worse "We do *not* fight. That was nothing.") you send the message that you are unwilling to be honest and that your child has done something wrong by telling the truth out loud. You imply that her perceptions are faulty, that it is not safe to wonder. You close a door.

How can you respond in a more helpful way? First of all, look at a particular question from your child's perspective. Chances are she does not mean to attack at all. Rather than reacting with anger, stop and think. What is she really asking? Psychoanalyst Theodor Reik called this listening with "the third ear." Others think of it as listening to the child with one ear and to God with the other. If a question is really upsetting, delay: "I'd like to think about that question a little bit before I answer. Let's talk about it after dinner."

Take a few minutes to ask yourself, "Why does this question upset me so much? What am I worried my child will find out? What am *I* uncomfortable with in my own life?" If your child asks about marital arguing, for example, and you are actually contemplating divorce, think through your feelings. You are probably angry, hurt, and confused about your spouse; you may be feeling guilty about the disruption and hurt the break-up of your household will cause your child. When the right time comes, you will help her cope with it. For now, be honest without burdening her with more information than she can handle. "Daddy and I were very angry with each other last night. Things aren't going too well between us." If she then asks, "Are you getting a divorce?" be honest. "Well, we are thinking about getting a divorce. Sometimes living together stops being a good idea and when married people can't get along they are better off apart. But we will always be your Mommy and Daddy and we will both always love you very much." (For more on this topic, see chapter four).

No matter how enlightened our answers may be, nothing we say will ever speak as loudly as our everyday *actions*. Most parents realize this. Unfortunately, though, we often conclude that the best policy is to try to present our child with a flawless image of ourselves. When she or he "catches" us in an inconsistency, we feel like hypocrites. As we shall see, if a child points out an ethical decision we've made that may not have been open and above board—even if it's something as mundane as driving over the speed limit—we are far better off acknowledging our error and correcting it than denying our behavior.

Easy Listening

1. Don't be so worried about finding the right answer that you neglect the value of being attentive. Active, involved listening deepens your bonds by reassuring a child that she can express her deepest feelings and that she *matters* to those who love her.
2. Be willing to explore together.
3. Don't be afraid to say, "I don't know."
4. Find time in your day for conversation when your child seems interested—at bedtime, over chores, walking the dog.
5. Avoid being intrusive. You're not doing therapy or a cross-examination. Let your child tell you as much—or as little—as she wishes.
6. If you're feeling defensive, ask yourself why a particular question upsets you.

Exploring Together

Try a storytelling "duet." Choose a familiar situation: "A little girl woke up one morning and found a big box in her room. What happened next?" As your child offers a suggestion, try to add *only* enough to help her move onto the next episode in the story. For example, if she says, "The girl looked at the box and tried to figure out what was inside," you might say, "And then she managed to pick it up and shake it." Your child may be enthusiastic about writing down the story and saving it. It's fun to hear how much your child has to say. And as you discover how you can listen and build on one another's creative thinking, you "rehearse" for questioning dialogue.

Listen to music and share your impressions. On a rainy day or whenever your child is at loose ends, make yourselves comfortable on the floor or among the sofa cushions and play an instrumental work on the stereo. (Try a symphony or chamber music—lively pieces such as Tchaikovsky's *Nutcracker* Suite, Rossini's *William Tell* Overture, Saint-Saëns' *Carnival of the Animals*, or Vivaldi's *The Four Seasons* are popular with children. Jazz, New Age pieces with environmental sounds, and ceremonial or dance music from around the world also get their attention.) Listen to one movement or section at a time and share your feelings and fantasies. Did the music make you feel happy, frightened, peaceful? Did it sound as though rain was falling? Give your child the opportunity to speak first, and let her know you appreciate her comments. A younger child may wish to dance along with the music. With a less verbal child, you may wish to try a variation on this activity. Bring out paper and crayons for yourself and your child and make swirls and dots of color on the page as you listen. After the music is over, invite your child to talk about his artwork and the music.

The Parent's Path

With your spouse or a friend, try mirroring each other's statements. Choose a topic, such as where you want to vacation next year, how your last visit with your in-laws went, what's going on at work, how you'd like to redecorate your home, the biggest spiritual question in your own life. Take turns speaking. When your spouse makes a statement, wait for him to complete a thought. Then, rather than offering advice or an opinion, repeat his in your own words. Ask if he feels you've understood him. Although you may find this exercise awkward or stilted at first, with practice you will discover it increases your ability to focus on another person's concerns—including your child's.

Think back to the most important or puzzling questions you asked as a child. Set aside twenty minutes or so. Find a quiet place. Take a few deep breaths. Stretch your arms and legs. Close your eyes. Picture yourself as a young child wondering, maybe firing away questions at your parents. If Communists are so bad, why does God send them babies? If God is everywhere, does that mean he's in my stomach? Can we send my baby brother back to the hospital? Try to remember why you asked the question—where you were at the time, what was happening—and the answer you received. How did you feel about it? Were you satisfied? Frightened? Bewildered? How would you answer the same question if your own child asked it today?

Do you listen to your own questions? The question that's on our mind when we wake up in the morning, says Sam Keen, tells us what *quest* we're on. Put a pen and paper beside your bed tonight and as soon as you wake up, jot down whatever you're wondering. Whether you're asking yourself if you're about to lose your job, whether to relocate, or if the day is likely to turn out to be a dull one, here is a question related to your life's journey. Keep a notebook to notice the questions evolving over time.

No matter how busy you are, make time to be alone, even for just fifteen minutes a day. Jog, meditate, swim, or spend time quietly listening to music. In regularly getting away from the hectic pace of your daily life and doing something for your inner self, you begin to come into contact with the still small voice within yourself. By doing so, you learn to hear the inner voice, and appreciate it, in others.

· 3 ·

The
Growth of
Wonder

The answers usually given to children in the
nursery wound the child's frank and genuine
spirit of investigation, and generally deal the
first blow at his confidence in his parents; from
this time onwards he commonly begins to mis-
trust grown-up people and keeps to himself
what interests him most.
　　—Sigmund Freud, *The Sexual Enlightenment*
　　of Children

A child's questions are signposts along the road of development. As they grow, our children ask different
questions—or approach the same ones in different ways—
because they think and feel differently about themselves,
their relationships with loved ones, and their place in the
wider world. Questions reflect several different, intertwin-
ing paths of development: cognitive, emotional, social,
moral, and spiritual.

Infancy

A cuddly, gurgling babe in arms seems a long way from asking difficult questions. *And yet the trust she is developing now—through skin-to-skin contact, dependable feeding, and loving responses to her cries—nurtures in her the deep awareness that she is at home in the world, that life makes sense.*

As we meet her needs and soothe her in simple ways—changing her diaper when she cries, burping her gently, learning when she wants to be held and when she wants to be put down—we nurture the first stirrings of *faith.* The kind of faith I mean is not equivalent to religious belief. It is the child's awareness of her being. When mother is absent, the baby does not fall apart. Even at this tender age, the baby knows she *is.* D. W. Winnicott, the British child psychoanalyst, called this early state of awareness and cohesiveness the infant's capacity for "going-on-being." He recognized that at any age the felt sense that we are individuals living our own lives is essential to human meaning-making. And so Winnicott described this early state as "a kind of blue-print for existentialism."

As parents, we nurture this fledgling faith in our children just by being *ourselves.* Parents, said Erikson, through the humblest tasks of everyday caregiving, "represent to the child a deep, an almost somatic conviction that there is a meaning to what they are doing."

By following our own instincts, we encourage a baby's natural inclination to share her feelings—the earliest "dialogue" between parents and children. She smiles for the first time, and we smile adoringly back. We come to recognize that she does not feel like playing when she averts her gaze, or sometimes even arches her body away from us.

By four or five months, the baby is beginning to show signs that she is *separate* from mother and other loving caregivers. From this point, through the toddler years, she begins to develop a sense of herself as a *person*, and to playfully explore the difference between "me" and "not-me." She explores her mother's face, body, and clothing, puts food into her mother's mouth, and, while eagerly discovering how to creep away, she frequently "checks back" to be sure mother is present. These "experiments," which not only teach the baby a new way of relating but teach *parents* a new way to relate to her, are the explorations that lay the groundwork for questioning dialogue between parent and child.

Even during the first year of life the baby is using her senses to explore the world on her own. Long before a child can even put her wondering into words, she experiments with her *body*—wiggling her toes, swiping at a mobile, flipping over. As we watch, we marvel at her surprising combination of *playfulness* and *determination*. How hard she "works" to pop her toe into her mouth, or arch her body against the crib mattress, or drop a ball from the highchair! When she can "exercise" that playful determination and eagerness to explore—with simple toys and household objects, from an infant seat with a view of household goings-on, or traveling in a backpack—she is well on the way to a lifetime of questioning.

Toddlerhood

Those first, shaky steps across the floor mark a new relationship between the toddler and the wider world. Now she can walk upright, a small person who gets around on her own in the land of giants. This is an exhilarating time, the beginning of her "love affair with the world," to use the psychoanalyst Phyllis Greenacre's happy phrase. The one- to two-year-old is eager to explore, and (despite her frequent explorations of things we'd prefer she stay out of) we share her excitement and joy. She is most comfortable exploring if caregivers offer a child-safe environment for her to investigate, and make themselves available without hovering. She needs both the freedom to wander and the confidence to know she can return to us to display her discoveries (a banana peel found under the sofa, a new way of playing with a toy) or just get a hug.

Toddlerhood not only marks the child's earliest locomotion but also the beginning of remarkable powers of language. By the second birthday, the child has gone from some fifty words to more than several hundred—often a spurt that occurs in a matter of weeks. Now she is speaking in simple sentences. Often the child's very first sentence is a question: "Whazzat?" ("What's that?') A simple way parents naturally help the process along is by supplying words in the course of the day's ordinary goings-on: "Do you want to go on the *swing?*" "Is Billy *sad?*"

Encourage your child to develop an inquisitive mind by responding to his observations and requests, even when they are difficult to understand. "Mah," he says, and you offer a cup of milk, repeating the world clearly: "Milk? Here's a cup."

If his request is impractical, affirm his assertiveness even when you need to say no. "Go outside," he demands, tugging at the front doorknob. "We can't go outside now," you might answer, repeating his words. Then suggest a simple alternative: "We'll go outside after lunch. Would you like to watch the birds out the window for now?"

Few parents find it easy to satisfy the toddler's almost simultaneous needs for closeness and exploration. One of the best ways is to read aloud together. Cuddling up on the sofa with a good book, we wander around the world together as we share the words and pictures. Don't worry about reading the text; encourage your toddler to point to the pictures and name them together.

As toddlers learn that their world has rules, they deepen their awareness that life makes sense. By toddlerhood a child reaches an important "emotional milestone" that marks a new way of approaching the world, according to the psychiatrist Stanley Greenspan. Now she is capable of organizing surprisingly complex social, emotional, and behavioral patterns that enable her to understand the "meanings" of things. She picks up a toy telephone and puts the receiver to her ear. She sees a comb and runs it through her curls. She brings *Pat the Bunny* to Mom and sits down, waiting to look at the pages together. She understands that both things and people have "functions." This, says Greenspan, is the beginning of a "conceptual" attitude toward the world—the idea that life makes sense.

In the process of discovering—by trial and error—the rules of the world around them, toddlers are developing the *inner* controls they will need to be independent. They begin to understand when to use the potty. They try, unsuccessfully, not to spill apple juice at the table. They explore the way a small cup fits inside a larger one, but a large one does not go into a small one. Learning rules is often frustrating and painful for both parents and child, of course, because not all rules are to the toddler's liking. He wants to be autonomous, and yet it is scary to be so separate from parents, who are so big and powerful. Mommy says it's time to end a playdate when the toddler is determined, body and soul, to make it last longer. On the other hand, the toddler is sure a sandwich "ought" to be cut in quarters, or diagonally, and is hard pressed to understand why Dad doesn't know the "rule" when he is fixing lunch. The toddler often dissolves in tears, or has a tantrum. Even in happy moments we may overhear him chant, "No, no, no, no, no."

The toddler's noisy struggle is a constant reminder that he is learning to do things for himself in an environment that often feels overwhelming. He is trying furiously to make his way alone in a world where he is small and outnumbered. Paradoxically, as he grows more separate from caregivers, he seems to have a stronger wish to share his experiences and feelings in words. By listening and offering support we encourage further exploration. One mother found her small daughter's constant tagging along annoying. The once-independent child suddenly seemed helpless. "You're a powerful girl," she said in exasperation.

The child burst into tears. "No, I'm not!" she wailed.

At that point, the mother told me, she realized that her daughter "understood things better than I did. She didn't want me to baby her. She wanted me to help her learn to cope in the big world. *That's* why she was following me around."

When a toddler feels angry or frustrated, he does not need to be punished or indulged, but to know that we recognize his feelings and can help him recover. "I know you would like to play longer because you were having such a good time," we can say when he is unwilling to end a playdate. "But it's time to go home now."

As the toddler learns to control his impulses, he builds self-confidence—even *courage*—the building-blocks of questions. All through life, the child will be asking questions about problems and realities that have loomed large in the eyes of human beings for millennia: love, death, right and wrong, God. If he is to have the strength and determination to keep on asking, he needs caregivers who can offer support and understanding now as he tests the workings of the grown-up world around him.

Preschool Age

Imagination and wonder are the hallmarks of the preschooler's inner life, as they will be until she is six or seven. The three- or four-year-old asks questions that sound surprisingly philosophical, and then proceeds to answer them with whimsical-sounding explanations that demonstrate her love of the richness of symbol and story. "Does God eat?" asked one three-year-old, who then promptly followed up with an answer: "Yes! Angel food cake!"

The preschooler asks questions with a passionate abandon that often amazes adults. Questions seem to come a mile a minute during this period, reflecting her growing assertiveness and initiative. She is intensely curious and eager to share her observations with adults. Now that she is growing more independent, she enjoys a complex social life among her peers, is eager to try new games and projects. She enthusiastically practices social relationships and explores mysterious realms in pretend play ("I'm the mommy, you're the daddy, let's have a baby").

Often the preschooler's questions sound sophisticated beyond her years—and, in fact they are. Your preschooler will be frustrated and discouraged if you give abstract or technical-sounding answers. Try to offer responses challenging enough to encourage her to make connections with her own observations, but not so far over her head that they leave her utterly bewildered.

If your preschool child asks, "Why is the sky blue?" she is not ready for a scientific explanation about the refraction of light. Her "Why" means "What for?" She is trying to understand the *purpose* of things. "The sky is blue because it is daytime," is an answer that makes sense to her for now. "If it were night, the sky would be black." She is still new to the idea of color itself, and is likely to be interested in the "sky blue" crayon in her art box, and in comparing it with the other blue crayons. She might enjoy painting a bright blue sky with fingerpaint. Logic is not a limitation she worries about now, and as you seek to answer her questions, you need not let it worry you, either. Her notions of cause and effect are fluid. She takes the explanations and stories she hears from loving caregivers and assembles them into a lively "collage" of fact and fancy. She projects her own dramatic feelings onto the world around her. Her joy and curiosity are intense, but so are her fears. Death, pain, and powerlessness visit in the form of vivid personified images—witches, monsters, the "bad guy" on a favorite television show. The darkness in her room at night seems to have a life of its own.

At this age, a child's questions come from the heart. For now the best responses are those that address her *feelings* about the topics that are on her mind. If she asks, "Are there ghosts in my closet?" simply *telling* her that there are none is not enough. She needs reassurance that you are nearby when she needs you, and that she can sleep with the light on.

Likewise, answering her questions about God, nature, and other imponderables in *words* fails to satisfy her need to develop an inner felt sense of the world around her. Her view of the universe is still egocentric, still a projection of her own fantasies, and she is particularly fond of toys that offer an opportunity to create and rule over a tiny universe of her own—a dollhouse, a pirate ship or castle, a home-made diorama set up in a shoebox.

The preschooler likes *making things* that embody the abundant world of his imagination. If he asks, "Will kid-nappers get me?" give him a playset with "good guys and bad guys," along with art supplies and dress-up clothes. He will explore his fears spontaneously through play, with chases, captures, and rescues.

Later on, he will be ready to explore fearful topics through dialogue. Until he is six or seven, he can find deeply satisfying answers to his questions in the world of play. Encourage him to let his imagination spin, and offer opportunities to listen to stories and have hands-on experiences in the arts and in nature. In doing so you help expand his vocabulary and the inner treasury of sensations, images, heroes, and villains that will enrich his questioning mind in the years to come.

The School Years

By the age of seven or eight, your child is likely to be more secretive about many of her thoughts and feelings. In fact, she seems to be less aware of them. This is the period known as "latency," when the expression of a child's sexual and aggressive drives takes a backseat to the growth of self-esteem and the acquisition of knowledge. Freud originally conceptualized the latency period as a time when children's instinctual drives were suppressed. Today it is widely ac-cepted that—as most parents would corroborate—sexuality and aggression are still very much present at this age, and easily stirred up when a child is overstimulated. Keep in mind that the calm demeanor of the school-age child does not result from the *absence* of strong drives, but is the result of a delicate *balance* between the instincts and the ever-strengthening ego that contains them. Children seem to behave more aggressively after watching violent television programing, for example. And you have probably seen your child, watching a couple kissing on TV, hide his face and moan, "Ewww!" or "Yuck!"

No matter how much you wish to be frank and open, approach sensitive topics with care. Children often demand hard facts at this stage, and speak with a seeming sophistication after years of media exposure to sexuality and violence. "Mommy, what's a 'mistress'?" I heard one small girl ask her mother after staring intently at a tabloid near the supermarket check-out counter. But hearing too much too soon can be overwhelming. *Our answers are helpful only when they help a child make sense of the world and feel empowered to cope with challenges.* Information alone is not enough. In fact, unless the child is ready to hear what we have to say, information may only upset her.

One mother recalled the day she told her eight- and ten-year-old children that she was pregnant. "They asked, 'How did that happen?' " she said. "So I started to explain—as I already had a hundred times—about the penis and the vagina and the egg and the sperm." Apparently the notion of this biological procedure actually taking place in Mommy and Daddy's bed was too much for the kids to imagine, particularly in light of the unexpected prospect of a new sibling demanding their parents' attention. "My son ran right out of the room, and my daughter hid under the table," said the mother. "They know just how much they can listen to."

Go slowly. As you answer a question, pay attention to signs that your child is getting anxious: If she abruptly changes the subject, gets distracted, or cracks a joke, know that she has had enough. Respect her need for privacy. In our culture, "denial" may be popularly considered a pathological state, but in school-age children it is a healthy way of coping. When in doubt, say less. If your child wants to know more, she'll ask again. Don't be surprised if she asks the same question repeatedly over a period of months and appears to have forgotten everything you told her last time. This frequently happens when children ask about topics they feel especially conflicted about, such as sexual intercourse and death.

School-age children's questions are best approached as "research projects." Inviting your child to speculate about possible answers works up to a point, but it can be frustrating to a child this age, who insists that you "get real." If she asks, "Who's richer, us or the President," and you try to come up with a philosophical definition of the word *rich* that includes love and spiritual well-being, she is likely to interrupt and insist, "But who makes more *money?*" Perhaps at no other time in life are human beings more clearly focused on learning "just the facts, ma'am." At this age, the spiritual *is* the material.

Because a child is eager to explore the world in very concrete, specific ways, parents often find they simply lack the facts and figures she wants. Instead of blushing and stammering, take the opportunity to help her expand her powers of observation and dig deeper. You don't need to have all the answers.

"Mom, what's the big boom?" one eight-year-old inquired.

"I realized he meant the big *bang*," his mother later recalled. "Unfortunately, I also realized that I knew next to nothing about it, except that it's the scientific account of how the universe started."

In chapter nine you will find a simple explanation of the "big bang," along with advice on how to enrich your child's life with mythic accounts of creation as well. But the most meaningful approach to a question such as this is to *incorporate shared investigation into everyday activities.*

This does not mean embarking on a frantic round of scaled-down physics experiments. Keep it low-key and natural. Know the difference between *supporting* your child's interests and *pressuring* her to get involved in a project. Stick to projects you and your child genuinely *enjoy.*

Buy a set of encyclopedias at a rummage sale. Next time you and your child go to the library, suggest a look at the science bookshelf to find a book he can read himself. Be willing to spend some time poring over reference books together, and if your library has a computer, get help using on-line reference materials.

Ask if your child would like to join the astronomy club at school, or buy a simple telescope. At this age he has the capacity and determination to work hard on a project and finish it.

Take a family trip to the natural history museum. Encourage your child to collect rocks and minerals and be sure he has a special shelf in his bedroom to display them (he is likely to spend long hours arranging and labeling his specimens).

Perhaps most important, help your child connect with troubling questions emotionally through literature and the arts. School-age children are less inclined than toddlers and preschoolers to share their feelings, and it is important for parents to respect their privacy needs. It's worth repeating that helping a child come to terms with an upsetting topic does *not* mean trying to probe her unconscious mind, or doing your own version of play therapy with her. Let her put into words only that which she wishes to express, and accept her "I forget" when she chooses to keep silent. This is her natural way of coping, of maintaining the equilibrium that characterizes a healthy school-age child.

But you can engage your child on a deeper level by helping her explore her questions *symbolically*. As her inner world is populated with heroes and villains, births and deaths, victories and defeats, she acquires a symbolic vocabulary that speaks the language of her deepest self. A nine-year-old may not be able or willing to express his feelings about being the underdog on the playground, but he can identify with—and feel empowered by—David's conquest of Goliath. An eight-year-old may be unable to speak about the thought of someone she loves dying, yet she can begin to come to terms with death and dying by reading *Charlotte's Web*.

If we think of questioning dialogues as parents' and children's participation in the oral tradition, there is no time in childhood when this is truer than during the school years. Family and local history, Bible stories, tales from around the world, biographies of pioneers and leaders: Sharing a rich collection of stories feeds the child's soul. Stories convey meaning through *action*. They speak to the heart of the school-age child, who tends to think in terms of the plot of a story, not its theme. Later on, as she moves toward adolescence, she will begin to wonder about the philosophical meaning *behind* events and experiences, and to challenge some early assumptions.

Adolescence

The adolescent not only *looks* different from her younger sibling, but she *feels* more intensely and *thinks* in much more sophisticated ways. Her challenging and often antagonistic questions reflect the inner turmoil she is experiencing along with changes in her mind and body. *She is struggling to puzzle out who she is and to find her place in the adult world, an enormous undertaking in light of the conflicting value systems all around her—not to mention the hormones raging within.*

Even as far back as the fifth century, Augustine summed up his own adolescence by observing, "And I became a problem to myself." The *self-consciousness* of Augustine's remark is typical of these years. Preoccupied with her own body and feelings, she takes it for granted that she is the center of everyone else's attention, too. And after all, not since babyhood has your child's body changed so noticeably in so short a time. Between the ages of eight and thirteen (for girls) or ten to fifteen (for boys), your child grows as much as a foot taller, and may gain twenty to thirty pounds. Body hair grows. She has her first menstrual period, he has his first nocturnal emission. His voice changes, and his testicles enlarge and drop. Her breasts enlarge and waist shrinks as hips and thighs fill out. Their skin gets oily. They're sweaty. No wonder adolescents wonder who they are! They can hardly recognize themselves, any more than we can.

This exaggerated sense of self-importance sometimes develops into what the psychologist and author David Elkind has called the "personal fable," or the adolescent's grandiose image of herself as unique, invincible, and exempt from all the rules that apply to ordinary mortals. No one in the world, it seems, has ever felt as intensely about life as she does.

And yet this is also a time of facing inadequacy and loss. The adolescent is no longer a child. It is time to begin to structure her own life, to move beyond the loving protection of home and family. She is not likely to confide this news to Mom and Dad, but the prospect of so much sudden growing up is bittersweet. She is sure she is too tall, that she will never have clear skin again. She is coming to understand that there is no turning back to the carefree days of childhood. She may sound cynical, or tough, yet underneath it all she is surprisingly sensitive.

The adolescent's newfound sophistication is a reflection not only of physical and emotional changes, but also of his tremendously increased capacity for complex thinking. Most of us are accustomed to thinking of adolescence as a period of emotional and sexual upheaval, but Piaget's research showed that this is a time of profound *cognitive* change, as well. Part of the reason he is self-conscious is that, for the first time, he is able to understand that others have thoughts of their own that are different from his. He can understand that definitions of right and wrong, for example, differ from one culture to the next. He has discovered the *subjective* self and subjective experience, in romantic love, politics, religion, and nature. He is increasingly capable of that which Piaget called "formal operations," or thinking about thinking. He can consider hypotheses, think theoretically, question assumptions. "The adolescent differs from the child above all in that he thinks beyond the present," wrote Piaget in *The Child's Concept of Number*. "The adolescent is the individual who commits himself to possibilities."

This capacity for theorizing is a valuable tool in the adolescent's quest for a place in the world. Deeply absorbed in her own inner life, she is struggling to connect her feelings and observations with life in adult society, a process Piaget described as "messianic," noting that one group of teenagers he studied were willing to confess to "fantasies and fabulations which several years later would have appeared in their own eyes as signs of pathological megalomania." She talks endlessly about music, movies, friends, school, politics, or religion, sounding surprisingly vague much of the time; yet in the process of talking she is honing her point of view, finding out what she thinks.

No longer content to understand the world from the perspective of parents and teachers, your child is picturing life as it should be in *her* eyes. By exploring with peers, she is developing beliefs of her own. Her idea of beauty becomes part of an aesthetic theory (likely to be based on the standards of the "in" store at the mall, or of her favorite rock group). Her search for meaning may take her on a religious or philosophical quest. She accuses adults of hypocrisy, yet at the same time her own idealism is rarely put to practical use.

Because she is wondering with such passionate intensity, questioning dialogue with an adolescent is usually an argument. Your adolescent is making it abundantly clear that you do not know how to talk, dress, or act with her friends. *You* wish she'd keep her room cleaner, get to practice on time, and wear only one earring per ear.

And as for conversation, it has turned into one long battle. For years you worried that when your child asked a serious question, you had nothing worthwhile to say. Now that she is a teenager, she regularly lets you know that you were right about that. "Whatever happened to my darling child?" wailed one father of a thirteen-year-old. She is becoming an independent thinker, and by debating she is defining her own positions. Her arguing is a new way of connecting with you. Like the infant who learns to stand by pushing the soles of her feet against your lap, she is practicing a new skill.

Don't be fooled into underestimating the importance of your role in questioning dialogue. Keep in mind that although she may not show it, she is eager to use you as a sounding board on big questions: Why is there war? Why does God let babies die? What does it mean to be a feminist? Her debating skills may be dauntingly well-honed. You can help your adolescent by trying to avoid facing off emotionally on your conflicting viewpoints, and instead, approaching discussion as *joint brainstorming*. Your adolescent does need clear guidance and firm limits to protect her physical and emotional health as she faces peer pressure on drugs, drinking, and sexual activity. Yet when you are arguing about basic values, try to allow room for differences of opinion about the *ways* in which they are held to. If your child complains frequently about her church or synagogue youth group, for example, and it is important to you that she participate in congregational life, set up a meeting with clergy or staff to discuss ways she could help make the program more meaningful. Explore other activities she might enjoy—volunteering on an outreach project, teaching small children, or joining a class for adult members of the congregation. If none of these approaches prove to be satisfying, offer her the opportunity to go with a friend to a house of worship with a livelier youth program.

These days your adolescent is saving many of her questions for other important people in her life—peers, a favorite teacher, coach, camp counselor, or member of the clergy. Yet for all her independence, she still needs you.

Questions and Your Child's Temperament

Although developmental guidelines can be helpful, it is important to keep in mind that children respond to their environment in individual ways. As adults, we all approach questions differently. Not surprisingly, our styles and preferences are evident from the very first days of life. The developmental theorist Stella Chess and her colleagues who pioneered in the study of temperament found noticeable differences even among *infants*—as parents have recognized for generations. Look into a hospital nursery and notice how one newborn is kicking furiously in her bassinet as others sleep placidly. Join a group of new mothers and hear how one infant eats and sleeps on schedule after the first few weeks, another is still up all night after a year. One infant is easily startled and cries at loud noises; her older sibling dozes through movies and transcontinental flights. Your toddler stumbles at top speed into a strange room, while her playgroup buddy clings to Mom's knees. From the earliest months children differ in their approaches to new situations, in their moodiness and intensity, their ability to concentrate, and their persistence and attention span. The overall pattern of behavior is the child's temperament.

Without even thinking about it, most parents naturally adapt to their baby's temperament. We recognize that a quiet baby needs a gentle touch, and his active sibling loves to be bounced and tickled. We learn how she tells us she is sleepy or hungry. Even when a baby's style is very different from a parent's, and seemingly incompatible, we usually manage to adapt.

As a child learns to speak, we come to recognize the unique ways temperament affects his approach to questions about life. As we grow increasingly aware of his personal style, we are better prepared to keep communication going.

If your child is *outgoing and direct,* chances are she asks a question point-blank, as soon as she thinks of it, and invariably challenges your answer. (When you're losing your patience, keep in mind that the child who fires one question after another is likely to be bright and alert.) Outgoing kids appreciate on-the-spot answers, and when you can't offer one they need help delaying gratification. Suggest a better time to talk. "I can't answer that question right now," you can say. "Let's talk about it while we're driving to the supermarket." Try to keep your agreement concrete. One father told his highly inquisitive four-year-old, "Let's limit questions to four an hour," not realizing that a four-year-old could not conceptualize time on a clock. By school age, be prepared for your child to be less forthcoming with questions. She is likely to be comparing notes with peers at school and in the park.

Shy children are, not surprisingly, more reticent about asking questions. Does your child approach a new play situation by standing outside a group and looking on for a while, then picking up a toy and playing alone until at last she seeks out one playmate? Maybe you've noticed that if you let her go at her own pace, she invariably ends up joining the fun with gusto. These children may bring up a troubling topic during an intimate moment—say, after a bedtime story. Like teenagers, they may "chew on" a particular worry for several days before mentioning it, write about it in a diary, or explore it in fantasy play. They may appear to ignore your answer until they respond the next day with a follow-up question. To talk about painful or frightening topics, they need time and space for low-key, one-on-one conversation with Mom or Dad. An informal setting—doing the dishes together, or walking the dog—is less intimidating than an "official" heart-to-heart talk. Try not to think of these occasions as opportunities to pry into the inner crevices of your child's soul. Keep your comments short, and know when to let the subject drop. Be available but not too eager.

If your child is particularly *active or difficult*, coping with challenging questions may seem like the least of your worries. "My child doesn't stay still long enough to have a conversation," one mother told me. A younger active child may find it difficult to express concerns verbally, and unless encouraged to do otherwise may simply lash out by hurting a playmate or throwing toys. Yet if you make it a point to spend quiet time together, encouraging your child to ask questions, you may be surprised to discover that you're helping him settle down and enriching your relationship. Build trust by setting firm but clear limits about the consequences of misbehavior, and try to avoid sarcasm or labeling him. Provide vocabulary to help him talk about feelings. Set aside regular time for *active* fun together. By school age you may notice that unusually active or difficult children ask questions right in the middle of a soccer game or one-on-one basketball.

Questions All Through Life

As a parent, you know that the process of growing up is richer and more complex than any developmental theory. In real life, growth is far from an orderly, linear process. Each of us grows up with particular experiences of family, community, faith tradition, a particular combination of temperament and talents, our own set of problems and challenges. Knowing developmental stages is helpful, but to respond sensitively to our children's questions, we need to honor another way of knowing. We need to hear the inner voice that reminds us that not all growing can be charted or diagrammed.

Rather than thinking of each stage of life as a step up toward mature adulthood, there is wisdom in recognizing that each stage has its riches. At times it is not at all clear that a young child's thinking is less "advanced" than an adult's. Is it lack of sophistication that makes it difficult for her to understand why we can't help the homeless person on the sidewalk? Developmental norms fail us when we are faced with explaining tragedy, or even the everyday news headlines. Knowing that a child's language is developing on schedule, or that she is in a particular stage of moral reasoning means little when we are faced with explaining a news report about an infant found in a dumpster, or the thousands of children around the globe who die each day of starvation. Healthy children can often ignore realities that are too painful to be grasped, thank God, and yet they are also capable of simple caring that astonishes and touches adults. There are blessings at each stage. Our children teach *us.*

Most of us spend our lives sorting through our experience and learning from our mistakes. Through the years we discover that some of our long-held assumptions and values no longer make sense, and still others are worth cherishing against all odds. "God instructs the heart," observed De Caussade, "not by ideas but by pains and contradictions."

Exploring Together

Encourage your child to keep an "I Wonder" scrapbook or folder. If she is old enough to write, invite her to collect her own questions. Challenge her to come up with as many innovative answers as she can. Include space for "research" materials—related newspaper clippings, stories and poems, bibliography.

Ask open-ended questions that stimulate your child's creative thinking. "How do you think people will cook dinner a hundred years from now?" "If Abraham Lincoln [or another historical figure your child has read about] were alive today, what do you think would most surprise him about the way we live?" "If our dog could talk, what would he say?" Don't be afraid to include questions that don't require an answer at all. "Close your eyes and imagine: What would it taste like to bite into an apple right now? Can you think of the sound of rollerblades on the sidewalk?" Rather than quizzing your child, ask her questions like this when they occur naturally to you—when your own imagination leads you to wonder.

The Parent's Path

Keep a notebook of your child's questions. Make a note of the date, the circumstances, and your response. Later on you'll enjoy looking back and remembering what they were wondering when. In the meantime, writing down the questions gives you an appreciation of the number and variety of the questions your child asks, and helps you become aware of subjects that seem to weigh heavily on her mind.

Think of the question you'd most like to ask an important person in your life. This exercise gives grown-ups a "taste" of childlike wonder. If you could bring up any question, what would you most like to ask:

> the President?
> your boss?
> your dog or cat?
> your ex-spouse?
> the IRS?
> your first love?
> God?

If you like, write down each question in the form of an imaginary letter. Now fantasize about the answer you might receive. (Make up a reply if you like, or, if you are doing this exercise with a partner, write "replies" to one another's letters.)

Ask yourself, What fact about my life would I least like my child to know about? Why? How does the event or behavior you have in mind contradict the values you seek to teach your child? Can you forgive yourself for the mistake? This exercise is *not* intended to encourage you to sit down *with your child* and "tell all." But acknowledging your mistake *to yourself*, or in prayer, is a meaningful and memorable opportunity to connect ideas with personal experience. You may find it helpful to talk it over with your spouse or a trusted friend.

Books

FOR PARENTS:

Erikson, Erik. *Childhood and Society.* W. W. Norton, 1963.

Fowler, Jim, and Sam Keen. *Life Maps.* Winston Press, 1978.

Frankl, Viktor E., *Man's Search for Meaning.* Washington Square Press, 1984.

Patterson, Dolly K., ed. *Questions of Faith.* Trinity Press International, 1990.

Piaget, Jean. *The Construction of Reality in the Child.* Ballantine Books, 1954.

FOR CHILDREN AND PARENTS:

Colum, Padraic. *The Children's Homer: The Adventures of Odysseus and the Tale of Troy.* Macmillan, 1918.

D'Aulaire's Book of Greek Myths. Doubleday, 1962.

Evans, Margaret Price. *A Child's Book of Myths and Enchantment Tales.* Macmillan, 1986.

Hamilton, Virginia. *The People Could Fly: American Black Folktales.* Knopf, 1985.

Healy, Jane M. *Is Your Bed Still There When You Close the Door?* Doubleday, 1992

Jaffrey, Madhur. *Seasons of Splendor.* Puffin, 1985.

Mayo, Gretchen Will. *Earthmaker's Tales.* Walker and Company, 1989.
Phelps, Ethel Johnston. *The Maid of the North: Feminist Folk Tales from Around the World.* Holt, 1981.
Russell, William F., ed. *Classic Myths to Read Aloud.* Crown, 1984.

Look for the *Boxcar Children* series by Gertrude Chandler Warner (published by Albert Whitman and Co.), C. S. Lewis's *The Chronicles of Narnia* (Macmillan), and Laura Ingalls Wilder's *Little House* books (published by HarperCollins)— all classics that portray a child's life as a journey and an exploration.

· 4 ·

Love

Every developing human child rests, like all developing beings, in the womb of the great
mother—the undifferentiated, not yet formed
primal world. From this it detaches itself to
form a personal life. . . . But this detachment is
not sudden and catastrophic like that from the
bodily mother. The human child is granted
some time to exchange the natural association
with the world that is slipping away for a spiritual association—a relationship.
                    —Martin Buber, *I and Thou*

"In the beginning is the relation," wrote Martin Buber.
Each of us come into the world as unique, separate
selves, and yet we were born to relate. From the earliest days
of life, babies respond to human faces, to a smile, to their
own mother's voice and milk. Long before they can put
their feelings into words, they show a readiness to *share*
them with caregivers in meaningful ways—through body
language, facial expressions, a variety of different cries.
Long before we and our children can *talk* over questions

about love, our everyday exchanges lay the foundation for relationships all through life.

Not all our moments together are blissful, needless to say. What a shock it is the first time a child shouts, "I *hate* you!" And yet, isn't this ambivalence one of her most important lessons about love? From the start she is learning to balance togetherness with separateness, and to cope with love and loss. Through it all she is encountering the *aliveness* of love.

Most of us learn about love the hard way all through life. "I *try* to talk about the challenges of love with the couples who ask me to officiate at their weddings," one member of the clergy told me, "but there's no getting through to them. They're all comatose." He shrugged. "Three years down the road when they wake up, I know I'll be seeing them again— only this time for counseling."

In our culture, as Erich Fromm observed in his classic work *The Art of Loving*, when we talk about love we usually have in mind *being* loved or lovable (i.e., physically attractive or charming), or *finding* an ideal love object (Mr. Right), or falling in love. *Rarely do we focus on learning how to love.* Through the challenges of family life we are learning about love as a verb, about what it means *to love*. We are learning how to live lovingly in community. "Love is not primarily a relationship to a specific person; it is an *attitude,* an *orientation of character* which determines the relatedness of a person to the world as a whole," wrote Fromm.

Our children spend many years knowing what it is to *be* loved, and understanding love as *need,* long before the idea of love as an enduring force of relationship has any meaning for them. They listen to fairy tales, they ask us to tell them how Mommy and Daddy met, they bicker. I asked one nine-year-old what love is and he shrugged. "I don't know. You *like* someone. Hugging and kissing and that stuff." He scowled. "Anyway, what are you *talking* about?"

The more willing we are to recognize love in all its complexity, the less likely we are to pass on unhealthy messages that echo the prevailing cultural myths—that romantic love conquers all, for instance. We need not worry that our answers are paradoxical or even out of reach. Human beings do not learn about love in the abstract: we wrestle with it, body and soul, for a lifetime.

Love is an adventure and a conquest. It survives and develops like the universe itself only by perpetual discovery.

—Pierre Teilhard de Chardin

The Growth of Love

In the everyday dance of childhood, the alternate moments of holding and letting go, our children experience the everyday mysteries of love. The most prominent theorists of human development in Western culture, from Erikson to Kohlberg, focus on the growth of *autonomy,* as though connectedness were somehow to be outgrown. Yet for thousands of years human beings have recognized that the road to maturity winds its way between independence and caring. As a number of theorists—feminists in particular—have observed, a fuller, more authentic understanding of development acknowledges the ongoing dynamic between individuality and interdependence, between love and aggression, that characterizes human life from the very beginning.

Although your child's questions about love may *sound* theoretical, often she is seeking reassurance of your steadfast affection. Not surprisingly, her needs change as she grows and develops. This is especially true during times of transition in her own life or in your family routine. You've probably noticed that when your child is going through a growth spurt or a change in schedule—joining a new class, for example, or starting summer camp—she asks questions about love. Changes are reminders that she is moving toward independence, that she is sometimes angry with parents, and even that she will one day outlive you.

During infancy, love is the joy of closeness, of skin-to-skin contact, of mutual recognition, of trust.

According to the pioneering infant research of Daniel Stern, by nine months a baby is aware of the "fit" between her own feelings and the expression of a caregiver. In one experiment, babies who had been upset about being separated from their mothers preferred to look at a sad face rather than a happy face. When parents are "attuned" to an infant's feelings—when they understand what a baby is telling them by his cry and by his facial expressions and body movements—and when they respond by letting him know they understand, in a way that he in turn can grasp, they teach him to trust. They are sharing with him the felt sense that he is loved. The baby is learning life's most important and for many people, sadly, most elusive lesson: that he is loved *because he exists*. This deep awareness is the seed of self-love. Without it, he can never truly love another. "Love thy neighbor *as thyself*," begins the great command of the gospels.

Yet even a baby is learning something about the ups and downs of love. You feed her, then put her down; she cries, and you pick her up. You cannot always soothe her, although you wear yourself out trying. Sometimes she screams herself to sleep. She is also learning to live with solitude: to know that she exists when you are not with her. She is developing the capacity to hold a mental representation of caregivers in her mind during their absences.

By the toddler and preschool years, your child is learning to see loved ones as whole people, people who sometimes give her what she wants, sometimes say no—people for whom she can simultaneously feel both love and anger.

She may be surprisingly clingy now, as she is learning that it is exciting to walk away from caregivers and explore the world, and yet frightening, too.

Parents during this often tumultuous time are alternately delighted with the toddler's growing independence ("She can *walk* while I carry the groceries!" one mother told me gleefully) and frustrated by her determination to be in control and do it *her* way. Yet by letting a child know that it is safe to be separate, that she can be her own person and still be loved, you offer a crucial lesson. She is beginning, as the psychoanalyst Jessica Benjamin has observed in *The Bonds of Love*, to see her mother as a separate, real person with human imperfections, rather than as an idealized, omnipotent being. This is an essential step if the child is to learn to love freely, to integrate love and aggression. "The idea that mother is or should be all-giving and perfect (just a kiss away from all-controlling) expresses the mentality of omnipotence," writes Benjamin, "the inability to experience the mother as an independently existing subject. . . . [H]ate has not been able to come forth and make the experience of love less idealized and more authentic." The child is no longer a baby. There is a wider space between you. Parent and child are learning a new way to love.

By school age the child is learning about relationships in the context of a life of her own, with an often-changing group of "best friends" and a clubhouse with a hand-lettered sign that reads, "No boys alowd."

On the playground the school-age child is learning the fun of making new friends, as well as the cruelty of being teased or left out. *She is learning to be cautious as well as trusting.* With siblings she is learning to stand up for her own needs, to take turns, to resolve the conflicts that inevitably arise even in the most loving families and communities. "I wish I was an only child!" she yells after an argument with her brother, and five minutes later we hear her asking him to go outside and play baseball.

Now that many of her lessons in love come from outside the home, questioning dialogue often brings surprises. "Mom, what's a pervert?" a six-year-old asked her mother one morning at breakfast.

"It's a person who does things with his or her body," replied her mother slowly, "that don't show love." She paused for thought.

The child's nine-year-old brother frowned. "No," he told his sister in a superior tone. "It's somebody like Madonna."

Peers and popular culture are important now, but the school-age child is increasingly aware of herself as a member of her *local community:* a faith tradition, a racial or ethnic group, a circle of family friends. This is an important time for her to learn the history and rituals of her own groups, and to enjoy belonging. To share in the traditions of family and faith is to learn that love lives on through generations, in our celebrations, stories, and achievements. And as a child encounters the challenges of getting along with people from other cultures, whose backgrounds and needs may seem startlingly strange, she learns that love means working toward common goals. This marks a step away from love as need and toward love as *giving*.

Love between parent and teen is a roller-coaster ride. Once she is a *teenager,* suddenly we discover that our very connections have turned into separations of sorts; that through the painful process of arguing with us about almost everything, she is struggling toward independence and an identity of her own in the wider world. A teenager spends more time consciously worrying about love than ever before, barraged by sexualized images of relationship in the media (not to mention her own hormones). Yet she seems less interested than ever in what we have to *say* about these subjects. "I had no idea that living with a teenager would be like living with a psychotic," one beleaguered father told me with a deep sigh. At this age the strength of our child's attachment to us can be measured by her angry protests against us, a dynamic that reflects, in the words of Terri Apter's *Altered Loves,* a moving account of female adolescence, "the bonds of loving hatred."

Sometimes, particularly during adolescence, a child asking about love seems to be testing parents: Do you really love *me,* the way I really am, for myself? This is an opportunity to point out that loving someone does not mean agreeing about everything. We respect one another's differences in areas that do not affect our basic values—tastes in clothing, say, or the music we enjoy. Sometimes, on the other hand, we need to take a difficult stand, to recognize that even true love has limits.

From his earliest days, even in the most loving, healthy home, a child learns that love relationships are a struggle. What lesson could better prepare him for the realities of life? To bring together our own feelings and needs with those of others, to learn to give and take, to speak and listen attentively, requires purposeful effort. "I've quit doing marriage counseling," a colleague told me once. "I can't take it anymore. Everybody wants to get their needs met and feel good. Nobody understands that a relationship is *work*."

No wonder children's questions about love often catch us off balance. They represent our children's efforts to integrate conflicting emotions, and to make sense of experiences that defy conventional logic. "If you love me, why do you spend so much time with the baby?" "If you and Dad got married and said you'd love each other forever, why are you separating?" "How can you say you love me if you won't let me do *anything?*"

As always, the uncertainty we feel as we struggle to respond to our children's questions is a starting point. It is a sign that we have let go of simplistic answers and are on the path to authentic dialogue. Now we can begin to speak from the wisdom born of our *experiences* of relationship in life—with family, partners, and friends—and to help our children do the same.

Family Love

When a child asks about the relationships in her household and extended family, she is seeking to understand how love works. She is exploring what it means to be close and yet be separate. She is learning whether she can get the respect and attention she needs from those closest to her, even when by talents or temperament she is different from others in the family, or less than perfect. She is wondering what it means to care for others she has a hard time loving—"bratty" siblings, intrusive aunts, children in distant third-world countries. She does not need to know all the details of family squabbles; she does learn by observing relationships that endure, year in, year out, through disagreement, change, and loss, the kind of steadfast, everyday affection the psychologist Robert Johnson calls "stirring-the-oatmeal love."

"Home," wrote the poet Robert Frost, "is the place where, when you have to go there,/They have to take you in." We think that if only our family life were perfect—if only everybody could stay married, not die, never argue, and eat dinner together every night—our children would be more secure, more trusting, more loving. But real-life family love, in all its tension and ambivalence, teaches children that they can cope with the ups and downs of relationship and still *belong.* No matter what shape your particular family takes, by listening to your child's questions and observations and responding to her needs for appreciation and affection, you help her grow up with a healthy awareness of her interdependence and with the wholeness and strength to find the love she needs all through life.

And yet our children also learn that an intrinsic part of everyday family love is loss. Parents say no. Siblings grow up and leave home. People grow old and die, or die young. Because those she loves do sometimes let her down, a child learns to cope with the truth that love always carries with it the possibility of loss and disappointment. Even the most devoted parents cannot protect a child from all pain. And yet by acknowledging a child's suffering—rather than evading it, or offering false reassurance—you offer a lesson about love that goes deeper than words. When you listen attentively to her feelings and show empathy, you let her know that you are with her even in the face of loss. Your presence tells her that even in the midst of her disbelief, hurt, and anger, she is still loved.

If you really love me, why won't you let me do everything I want?

I do love you. I know you'd like to do this your way. I believe you have the right to make your own choices about a lot of things. People who love each other respect each other's right to make choices. But on this issue, I'm not willing to negotiate, because I don't think you're ready to make a responsible decision. Knowing when to make that judgment and standing by it even though you're angry with me is part of being a loving parent.

If you love me, why do you yell at me?

I do love you very much. Most of the time I try to talk to you in a calm way, so that you can listen and understand. But sometimes when you don't pay any attention to my calm talking, I raise my voice. All kids tune parents out sometimes. If this is a source of discord in your house, now is a good time to work together on a new approach to your child's "deaf ears." Sit down and plan on a signal that alerts your child to the fact that you are saying something important and expect her attention. You might tap her on the shoulder, for example. Or you can agree on a special "formal announcement": "Okay, folks, I have something important to say and I only want to say it once. Are you listening?" Wait for a reply before you talk further. Some kids find it amusing to use walkie-talkie language: "Do you copy?" "Roger."

Once in a while I'm feeling cranky or sad. Maybe it's been a bad day at work, or I have a lot on my mind. I try to remember to tell you I'm feeling grouchy on those days. It's not fair for me to yell at you when the problem is really how I feel and has nothing to do with you. I love you and I want you to know that you deserve to be treated with respect.

If you love me, why did you spank me?

I was wrong to spank you because, as you know, I don't believe hitting people is a good way to show anger or solve problems. I love you and want to treat you with respect. I'm sorry for spanking you. When you and your child have calmed down, sit down together and make a "contract"—verbal or written—that clearly spells out the negative consequences of specific misbehaviors. For example, you will not walk into her room when it's messy, even to get dirty laundry out of the hamper; if she wants clean clothes she'll have to tidy up. Next time you get angry you can remind her of your agreement. When you are tempted to spank, call "time out" and send your child to her room. And if you are stressed out and at wit's end more often than you'd like, take care of yourself: try to spend twenty minutes reading a novel, taking a bubble bath, or chatting on the phone with a friend without talking about kids or work.

Helping a child learn to cope with everyday disappointments is different from teaching her to "understand" neglect or abuse, of course. If your child is suffering from a lack of attention, or from hurtful behavior, she needs support and protection or she will begin to associate love with pain.

If Mommy loves us, why doesn't she take care of us?

Mommy does love you, but when she is drinking [or de-

pressed or using drugs] she can't even take care of herself. It doesn't have anything to do with you, and you didn't make it happen. It's okay for you to be angry about it. You can tell me your feelings whenever you want, or you can talk to [name a school counselor or your child's therapist]. *I hope Mommy will be different now that she is getting some help.* [If she is not getting help, say you hope she will.] *She is sick. In the meantime, I am doing the best I can to take care of you. Please tell me what you need. I love you very much.* If the neglect or abuse continues, contact 1-800-4-A-CHILD, or seek family therapy (1-800-374-2638 for the American Association for Marriage and Family Therapy; 1-212-741-0515 for the National Association for the Advancement of Psychoanalysis). Find a support and information group for your child at school or through Al-Anon or your local Alliance for the Mentally Ill.

To be aware of our own ambivalence and hurt without poisoning our child with them, to recognize our child's pain, to offer support, and to tell the truth: Often this *is* the best we can do. "Why doesn't Daddy call more often?" one teenaged girl asked her mother after a bitter divorce. "How am I ever going to be able to trust men when my own father just leaves town and doesn't come back?"

The girl's mother was silent for a few minutes. "I felt so guilty," she told me a few days later. "I wanted to tell her how furious I am with him for being such a bastard, but I knew that would be wrong. Finally I told her I didn't understand why her father was acting that way, and that I know *all* men aren't like this. And I said I knew how painful it was for her, and that I know it's going to take her a long time to learn to trust. I wish I could have said something more wonderful or inspiring, but it's the truth. It was the best I could do."

And it was no small thing. This mother offered the gift of thoughtful reflection on life experience, the only meaningful source of wisdom and hope. Each time our child asks a question about family relationships, our honest, compassionate response helps her add a new picture to her "emotional photo album." Some of the pieces are faded, or even torn. Others are sharp and bright. Through the years, as we help her put together the joy, sadness, and conflict that make up any childhood and any household, we help her know the truth—the endlessly rich, often contradictory truth—about family love.

Good news about siblings: Although much of the advice written for parents on sibling relationships focuses on rivalry, there is a great deal of evidence to show that siblings naturally feel loving and protective toward one another. As we help our children learn to get along with their brothers and sisters, we teach them a great deal about love of neighbor. This seems to be true when parents *teach* children empathy. In 1982 Judy Dunn of Penn State University, who frequently studies the development of morality and caring in children, reported the results of an interesting three-year study. She and her colleagues found that if mothers talked about a newborn's feelings and needs with an older brother or sister, he or she was more likely to be affectionate with the baby, to help out, and to play with her. Three years later, the researchers found, the pattern continued. Older children who had been taught to empathize were more likely to share toys or candy, and to comfort a younger child in distress. At the same time, the younger children at the age of fourteen months were more social with their older siblings than babies in other families.

When your child asks sibling questions that sound decidedly less than loving ("Can you send Tommy to his room?"), it may be reassuring to remember that the ambivalence inherent in our relationships with our brothers and sisters is one of life's best lessons in reconciling love and anger. Part of learning to love is learning to assert your own power appropriately. What better school for this lesson than the sibling relationship? By helping siblings resolve conflict, we teach them to distinguish between *true intimacy* (in which individuals express their needs clearly and respect their differences) and *emotional fusion* (the denial of differences for the sake of a "togetherness" which does not meet either person's true needs). The more constructively you help your children learn to cope with their conflicting feelings and speak to one another truthfully and peaceably—rather than depend on you to intervene and force a solution or just tell them to stop bickering—the more you equip them for healthy relationships with others all through life.

Who do love more, me or the baby?

I love you both with all my heart. The baby needs my help in many ways right now—to get food, to go to sleep, to have her diaper changed, even to move around the house. I wonder whether you think that since I pay so much attention to the baby I love her more than you right now. I remember how when you were a baby I held you in my arms, I breastfed you, I rocked you to sleep and sang to you. I even changed your diapers! (You might suggest looking at your older child's baby pictures together during the baby's nap, when you can devote your undivided attention to it.) *Now that you're bigger,*

I love seeing all the wonderful things you've learned to do. I'm proud of you when you pour your own milk, and ride a tricycle, and get dressed all by yourself. I love playing checkers with you. I take care of you in different ways now—I take you to nursery school, I give you things to play with, like playdough and blocks—and I love doing those things, too. Even though I'm very busy with the baby, I'm going to make sure you and I have some special time every day for just the two of us.

Can we send the baby back to the hospital?

The baby is part of our family now. He is your little brother. It certainly is a big change having him around, isn't it? He makes so much noise and keeps Mommy and Daddy very busy. Sometimes I think we'd all like a break. I guess you would. I'm glad you told me your feelings. He won't always be this much work. But anyway, I'm making sure you and I have some special time together every day. I love you. You might read *The Berenstain Bears' Little Sister*. Also, give your child a family playset (like the ones manufactured by Playmobil or Fisher Price) that includes an older sibling and a baby. Don't interpret his play; just let him mull over the new shape of his family.

Why is my sister such a brat?

You're angry with her right now. In a family we all get angry at one another sometimes. Your sister did something mean to you. I don't blame you for getting mad right now, and I am glad you are using words to express your feelings. You don't have to play with her right now if you don't want to. But I hope when you're ready you will tell her how you feel and the two of you can agree on a way of playing you both *enjoy.* By affirming your child's verbal expression of anger and en-

couraging her to work toward a resolution of the conflict—
rather than telling her to be quiet or intervening to settle the
argument—you let her know that appropriate anger is part
of a loving relationship, and you empower her to assert her
needs.

Can I have a baby sister?

Mommy isn't pregnant right now.

*Mommy and Daddy aren't planning to have a baby
right now.*

*Mommy and Daddy don't expect to have any more chil-
dren.*

*Mommy and Daddy would like to have another baby, but
we're not sure if that will happen. We are seeing some doctors
who are trying to help us have a baby.*

*Mommy and Daddy are very excited that we're going to
have another baby, but we don't know whether it will be a boy
or a girl. Whatever the baby turns out to be, we'll love it
anyway.*

*The doctor checked the fetus in Mommy's belly and found
out it's a boy. So you're going to have a baby brother! I know
you were hoping for a sister. I wonder what you can think of
that will be fun about having a brother.* Mention other baby
boys he knows, or friends who have baby brothers. Be sure
to avoid setting up unrealistic expectations by implying that
the newborn baby boy will be ready to play baseball. Tell
your child that all babies love cuddling and stroking. And as
they get older, they will share many things—books and
movies and ballgames.

The Extended Family

Children's questions about relatives and in-laws often touch on sore points, don't they? And yet for a child, as authors from Proust to Frances Hodgson Burnett have shown us, the extended family is populated with all of humanity. In learning about family obligations our children experience love in *action* over the long haul—something very different from the happy-ever-after feeling they hear in fairy tales.

Although your child is likely to be curious about family squabbles, involving her in the details is likely to be upsetting. On the other hand, by excluding her entirely you deprive her of a model of everyday conflict resolution, and she is likely to pick up the hostility on some level anyway. When your child asks about a disagreement with relatives, reassure her that all families face conflict and try to work together to resolve them.

One of the challenges of answering questions about the extended family is that our ideas and customs differ not only from family to family but also from one ethnic group to another. What's the "right" amount of closeness? Who are more important, friends or relatives? Which rites of passage do you celebrate? What role does a married couple play within the extended family? How are elderly people cared for? Your assumptions and concerns about extended family connection and loyalty probably differ from those of your spouse, your friends, and even other members of your extended family. Your child's lessons about family love are conveyed in the context of your particular way of life.

When your child asks a question about your family or in-laws, you may need to learn to be a "culture broker." Keep in mind that the same situation or behavior can have very different meanings from one culture (even one *household*) to another. Don't be surprised if your child wonders why your side of the family follows one set of customs and ways of interacting and your in-laws are very different. Help her make sense of the behavior. Rather than simply telling your child *how* people in your family do things, try to focus on the *values* behind your family's behavior. It helps to stop and ask yourself, "Why do we do things this way?" or "How do I really feel about this particular problem?" This is challenging but important, because children have an uncanny ability to pick up on our unspoken conflicts.

Why do I have to visit Grandma in the nursing home?

I know it's a little scary for you to visit. There are lots of people in wheelchairs, and many of them look very sleepy or sick, and Grandma isn't very well. Grandma looks forward to our visits and her conversations with us. She likes to read and watch TV, and she gets good care from the nurses and doctors there, but she wants to tell us about her aches and pains and hear all about what we're up to—the movies we've seen, your school and soccer games, my work. We all need to know that people we love care about us. Encourage a younger child to bring along art projects and other treasures to show off to Grandma. If your child is very anxious about the visits, ask nursing home personnel if you can visit in greater privacy away from other residents, or consider taking your child less often.

Why don't we get together with Uncle George anymore?

I know you miss Uncle George very much. Right now, for reasons that are private between us and Uncle George, we aren't seeing each other. I hope that someday we will be able to resolve our differences and get together again.

or

Everybody feels angry at or sad about their family some-times. We're always family. But Uncle George feels so angry that he doesn't want to see his family right now. I'm very sorry he feels that way because I love him very much, even though there are things about him I don't like at all. I hope that some-day soon we will get together again. You might wish to share the Biblical story of Jacob and Esau, which culminates in the deeply moving scene when the two brothers reunite and Esau runs to Jacob and forgives him. The complete story is told in Genesis 27–33, or read the adaptation in *The Adven-ture Bible* or *The Picture Bible* (see page 227).

Why do I have to play with my stupid baby cousin?
He's part of our family and he enjoys playing with big kids like you, just like you've always enjoyed playing with other big kids. Name an older cousin or a neighborhood friend whose company your child enjoys.

Why did you get mad at Grandma?
The subject we're disagreeing about is something that con-cerns me and Grandma, and I am not going to discuss it with you. I will tell you that mothers and their children don't al-ways agree about everything—you and I don't, and Grandma and I don't. Sometimes we get angry at each other. But we try to work out our differences, and we still love each other.

Romantic Love

Unlike generations past, we live in a society where the awareness and expression of sexuality is encouraged. Sex isn't dirty anymore. But in the media to which our children are exposed—television commercials, magazines on the check-out line—they see image after image of sexuality *without emotional content*, as something *separate* from the rest of life.

"Mommy, why is that lady's shirt unbuttoned?" I heard a preschooler ask in the supermarket, pointing to copies of *Cosmopolitan* on the magazine rack.

"Umm, I'm not sure. She must think it looks good that way," stammered her mother.

"But why would she let so many people see her breasts?" the little girl persisted. At this point the mother changed the subject by offering the child a candy bar.

Children are fascinated by body parts. Our culture introduces children to sexuality through the commercial display of body parts. *If we talk about body parts and the biological processes of reproduction without mentioning the emotional content of sexuality, we fail to offer the greatest lesson in love. We fail to teach her the true power of her erotic nature when it is one with her whole, spiritual self.*

Traditionally, myths and stories about sexuality have always reflected this powerful connection. By understanding erotic energy as the life force that links us with nature and the universe, our most ancient stories have helped people struggle toward ultimate questions of meaning and connectedness. Eros, according to early Greek mythology, was one of the four original gods who created life by piercing the "cold bosom of the Earth" with his life-giving arrows.

Through our erotic power, we reach out to the world creatively. "The questions about sex that the child asks are . . . not—at a fundamental level—about sex at all," wrote Ernest Becker in *The Denial of Death*.

> When the parents give a straightforward biological answer to sexual questions, they do not answer the child's question at all. He wants to know why he has a body, where it came from, and what it means for a self-conscious creature to be limited by it. He is asking about the ultimate mystery of life, not about the mechanics of sex. . . . We might say that modern man tries to replace vital awe and wonder with a "How to do it" manual.

Focusing on the mechanics alone misses the child's deepest needs. Very young children, whose minds are filled with the wonder and mystery of things, sometimes even "forget" or refuse point-blank to *believe* the "facts of life." If we insist on prematurely telling all, they find us intrusive. "My daughter was asking one question after another about childbirth," the mother of a five-year-old told me. "Finally I decided to show her a very tastefully photographed picture of a birth, with the baby's head emerging. My daughter took one look, burst out laughing, and told me, 'That's not *real!*'" School-age children, who explore the world that they can see and touch, look in vain for concrete evidence of a sperm or an egg. And yet at this age what is "real" to a child are the creation stories that tell of human beings created out of dust, or from the sea, and family histories that tell us about the people we come from—stories that capture the child's felt sense of connectedness with all life. If our answers to questions about love and sexuality can help her maintain this deep awareness, rather than contribute to the split between soul and sexuality that predominates in our culture, we discover that the whole world *is* contained in the drama between sperm and egg.

Children learn about romantic love and sexuality from all their relationships. During *infancy and toddlerhood,* as we lovingly attend to their physical and emotional needs, from feeding to diapering to hugs, we care for body and soul.

By *nursery school and kindergarten age* children are acutely aware of their sexuality. If they see Mom and Dad kissing in the living room, though, they're likely to shout, "Stop sexing!" and "Sex patrol!" They themselves are often highly assertive and affectionate. When parents are understanding—neither shocked by their unconsciously se-ductive displays nor seductive in response—we help our children integrate their strong drives into their whole, grow-ing selves and into healthy relationships.

Why don't I have a penis?

Men and boys have penises. Girls and women have most of our sexual organs inside our bodies. In here [show her] *you have ovaries, with thousands of eggs in them. They've been there since you were born. Inside we also have a uterus, the place where a pregnant woman carries her fetus.*

You have many special parts you can see. When you grow up, you will have breasts bigger than the ones little girls have. If you have a baby they will make milk to feed him or her.

The area between your legs is called the vulva. It has a sen-sitive part in front, the clitoris. Your child has undoubtedly already discovered this, and may think of it as "ticklish." *Lower down are the labia, which are like two "lips" that lead into a passageway called the vagina.* With a five- or six-year-old, you can say that the vagina is the place babies come out of; since she can hardly see an opening at all, be sure to mention that it stretches a great deal and then gets small again after the birth.

Why can't boys have babies?

Boys help make babies from their sperm, which unites with the egg. But boys can't be pregnant because they do not have a uterus to carry a baby in. After the baby is born, though, the father can hold and feed and bathe and love the baby just as much as the mother can.

Is my penis big enough?

Yes. Boys have penises of different sizes. As you get older, your penis will grow along with the other parts of your body. If your child has seen his father's penis—in the shower, changing clothes, etc.—he may be feeling intimidated, especially because a young child is short enough in stature to see adult genitals close-up, at eye level. Many parents choose to refrain from nudity in front of their children by the time their children are three or four.

Can I marry Daddy?

Daddy loves you very much. But Daddy's already married to Mommy [or Daddy's a grown-up man]. When you grow up you'll meet a man you like, and you two will get to know each other, and he will realize how wonderful you are and love you just the way Daddy loves Mommy.

What's sex?

Sex is a word for a special kind of closeness between a man and a woman. They kiss and hold and touch each other, and

*the man puts his penis between the woman's legs and into her
vagina. It feels good. People call it "making love." It is the way
mommies and daddies make babies.* By presenting sex not
only as a biological process that leads to babies, but as lovemaking, you help your child connect it with her emotional
life (and avoid suggesting that Mommy and Daddy have
only "done it" once or twice). Don't be surprised, though, if
her reaction is "Yuck!" or if she asks the same question
again frequently, as if she never heard your answer the first
time.

Did you love anybody else before you met Daddy?
Yes, I did, but not like Daddy.

or

*Yes, I did. We didn't get married because we weren't ready
to make such a big decision. After your Daddy and I got to
know each other for a while, we did feel ready and I'm glad
we did.*

or

*Yes, I did. We didn't get married because having strong feel-
ings about someone is not the same as thinking they will be a
good partner to have a home and children with. Your Daddy
and I have a lot of the same ideas about what's important to
us and how we want to live, and that's why we decided to
share our lives as married people.*

During the *school years*, through friendships, hobbies,
school, and sports, children learn to integrate their emotions with life in the real world. For the most part, aside
from bathroom humor and a fascination with four-letter
words, sexuality has become less of an explicit focus. None-

theless, during these long days of collecting baseball cards, doing gymnastics, and learning astonishing numbers of facts, your child is growing in her capacity to form mature relationships. She is learning to delay gratification, to hold onto a thought and understand that thought is different from action. When children have the opportunity to gain in strength and steadiness through the time-honored joys of childhood—rather than starting to date at an early age—they are better prepared to cope later on with the pressures of adolescent and adult love.

How often do you and Daddy "do it"?

Making love is one of the private, personal things Daddy and I share. I don't feel comfortable answering your question. It's important to set limits when your child asks a question you don't wish to answer. Keep in mind that she does not need to know everything about your private life (and hearing too much will only make her anxious). Her most important lessons about physical love come through your relationship with her, and the everyday affection she observes between you and your spouse—in the kitchen, taking a walk, when one of you is under the weather.

A younger school-age child is likely to equate Mom and Dad's estimated sexual encounters with the number of children in the family; you may wish to explain that lovemaking is something grown-ups do as part of their special time alone together, not only to make babies.

I heard you and Daddy fighting. Do you still love each other?

I know it's scary for you when we get so angry. I hope you know our arguments aren't about you. They are about things that concern me and Daddy. Daddy and I both love you very much. Daddy and I love each other, too. But sometimes we don't understand each other very well. And sometimes we don't agree on how to do things. When we are feeling very tired, or hurt, we end up shouting instead of discussing our problems in a reasonable way.

Later on, when we feel calmer—and sometimes that doesn't happen until later in the evening after you're in bed—we talk about what's bothering us, and we try to find ways to work out our problem. As you know, we both think it's important to learn to solve problems peacefully, and Daddy and I are going to make a special effort to do that more often in the future.

Are you and Daddy getting a divorce?

If you are not in the process of ending your marriage, see the answer to the previous question. Because your child has many schoolmates whose parents are divorced, don't be surprised if this question comes up after an occasional argument.

If, on the other hand, you are actually contemplating a separation, take some time to think through your feelings before answering your child. Although you are angry, hurt, and confused, know that you can help your child cope with the break-up of the household. But this will take time. For now, you need to be honest without burdening her with more information than she can handle. *Daddy and I were very angry with each other last night. Things aren't going too well between us.*

If she persists with the question, try to be truthful but reassuring. *We are thinking about getting a divorce. Sometimes married people decide that living together is not a good idea, that when they can't work out their differences anymore they'd be better off apart. But we will always be your Mommy and Daddy and we will both always love you very much.* (For more questions and answers on divorce, see page 88.)

Is love forever?

To love someone is something we choose to do. It's not just a feeling. Sometimes people fall in love and later change their minds about each other as they get to know each other better. They felt attracted to each other, but they didn't really love each other. To love somebody is to be willing to do the hard work of getting to know them, listening to them, and letting them know what is important to you. Sometimes two people love each other and one person does something very hurtful or uncaring. The other person might be willing to forgive them. But if things don't get better and they can't rebuild trust between them, love dies.

But we can always find love in this world when we know we need it. Mom and Dad love you, friends love you, brothers and sisters love you, and God loves you.

Can men marry men, and women marry women, or do only men and women marry each other? What's "gay"?

Usually men marry women and women marry men. Most people fall in love and decide to get married to people of the opposite sex—men with women, women with men. They are called "heterosexual." People who are gay, or homosexual, are attracted to people of their same sex. When they choose a partner, a homosexual man chooses another homosexual man and a homosexual woman (lesbian) chooses another homosexual woman.

We don't know why some people are heterosexual and others are homosexual. Many scientists believe we are born with a tendency to be one way or the other. Being gay is not a disease. It's not contagious.

It's sad and wrong that many homosexuals feel ashamed of their feelings and are treated badly by other people because of the way they are. Even though we are different in this way, heterosexuals and homosexuals share a lot. We both have the capacity to love other people in a responsible way. We have talents and energy to contribute to our world. And we are human beings God made and loves. You might name an openly gay or lesbian acquaintance, friend, or relative you and your child respect: *Uncle John is gay. Can you imagine not thinking he's wonderful, just because of that?*

Keep in mind that your child may be asking this question after hearing about—or engaging in—experimentation with a friend of the same sex. *All people have warm, loving feelings toward friends, teachers, and relatives of the same sex. Most children are very curious about each other's bodies. Loving someone of the same sex—or even being curious about a friend's body—is not the same as being homosexual. Most people have some feelings for the same sex but are basically heterosexual. A person who realizes over a period of years that he or she only wants love relationships with people of the same sex is basically homosexual. That's something a person can only really know for sure as a grown-up.* Let your child know he or she can always find someone to talk to. And know your limitations. If this is a recurring question your child may benefit from a conversation with a trained professional. *I'm always glad to answer your questions as best I can. I love you very much. Maybe you'd like to talk to a special helper called a counselor or therapist who knows how to listen very carefully and can help you understand your feelings.*

For the adolescent, romantic love and self-discovery go hand in hand. The glow of falling in love—that heady feeling portrayed in Disney ballroom scenes from *Cinderella* to *Beauty and the Beast*—fulfills the teenager's need to learn who she is by seeing herself reflected in the eyes of another person. To varying degrees adolescents are exploring the connection between sex and love, and the role of responsibility in a relationship. However, *you* feel about teen sex, your teen needs to learn that birth control is an essential part of responsible sexual activity. ("Children shouldn't have children," one mother told her adolescents.) Yet your adolescent also wants to know much more.

As you respond to her questions, keep in mind that sexual issues are part of her overall struggle with self-esteem. As she worries about her attractiveness and popularity, she is wondering whether there is a place for her in the world of relationships. Outside the context of home and family, she has little opportunity to hear that sex is one aspect of intimate sharing between two strong people who care deeply about each other. Abstinence during the teen years is recommended by many educators, because although children at this age are *physically* ready for sex they usually lack the *emotional* strength to deal with the powerful bonds of a genitalized relationship. As out of touch with today's reality as that may sound, in 1992 Dr. William Roper, director of the Centers for Disease Control, pointed out that the Surgeon General's 1964 *Report on Smoking and Health* led to a noticeable change in attitudes and behavior about smoking, and that AIDS awareness may have a similar impact on sex—if parents and educators approach the issue wisely. "Young people need to get the message to postpone involvement in sexual activity. We need to make sure that we are not simply engaging in puritanical preaching but are striving to create a new health-oriented social norm that allows teens to feel comfortable in choosing to refrain from sex."

What's safe sex?

"Safe sex" isn't really the right way to put it. Sexual contact is only safe with no exchange of body fluids—semen, menstrual blood, or vaginal fluids. Sex play that doesn't involve exchange of fluids (kissing, petting) is the only safe sex. Using a latex condom, especially if a woman partner uses a spermicide (which kills HIV) is safer sex, but it's not fail-safe. (For answers to questions about AIDS, turn to chapter six.)

Can you be in love with two different people at the same time?

Most of us know what it means to have strong feelings for two people at the same time. For grown-ups, deciding to have a love relationship is different from just having feelings. To really love each other means to enjoy doing fun things together, to try to understand and care for each other, to work to solve problems, and to trust each other—which is hard to do if you're really involved with another person.

Before you can get that serious about one person, you need to know them pretty well. You also need to know yourself pretty well, and what's really important to you. One way to find that out is to start by going out with different people.

Will I ever have a girlfriend?

People have their first girlfriend or boyfriend at different times. You are a wonderful person with so many nice qualities [name them—nice-looking, sense of humor, thoughtful, smart, etc.] *that I am sure before you know it a girl you like will come along who appreciates you.*

How does it feel to be in love? How do you know when you are in love? Do you think Brian really loves me? How can you tell when a relationship is real?

Sometimes this question is a way of asking, "Am I ready to have sex with my boyfriend?" If you have not discussed contraception with your child, now is the time.

No one can answer this question for another person, but by briefly offering a down-to-earth picture of a loving relationship, you can counteract the prevailing cultural myth that romantic love solves all problems and meets all needs. You can be most helpful to your child if you speak from your own experience.

I remember when I first got to know your Dad. We went out a few times, we spent a long time talking, we realized we enjoyed a lot of the same things [sports, movies, music, etc.]. I had a good time when I was with him, and he was nice to me. When problems came up, we listened to each other and talked about them. We didn't always agree, but we cared about each other's thoughts and feelings. I knew your Dad couldn't solve all my problems, or make my life easy, and that I couldn't do the same for him. We grew into a partnership. And even though I had strong feelings about Daddy pretty quickly, it took time for us to be sure we really loved each other. If you don't have such positive memories to share, think of two friends or relatives who have a healthy relationship. Point out some of the positive aspects, including the way this couple have made it through ups and downs. Emphasize that in a truly loving relationship, both partners care about and are nice to each other.

Divorce

Why are the Smiths getting divorced?

I don't know the details. Most of the time we don't know very much about other people's marriages. But I do know that when people decide their marriage isn't worth working on anymore—maybe because they've tried for a long time and just haven't been able to solve some big problems, or maybe because they don't realize how much work a marriage takes— they decide to split up.

Is it my fault you're getting a divorce?

You didn't cause our divorce, and you couldn't have prevented it. We are getting a divorce because we think it is the best thing for me and Mom. We have been having a lot of problems and even though we have tried to get along better, Mommy and I can't live together anymore. But we loved each other when you were born, we have always loved you, and we always will love you. Children of divorce almost inevitably fantasize about reuniting their parents; be sure to let your child know that this decision is final. If your break-up has come as a result of quiet tension, help your child understand that anger is not always noisy. Don't reassure her that now things are going to better for the whole family; she will find the separation painful, no matter how stressful your home has been, and she needs to grieve. Even if your spouse is the initiator of the divorce, avoid blaming him or her for breaking up the household. And be prepared to answer the same questions again and again as your child grapples with her feelings about the changes.

If you've stopped loving Mommy, does that mean you could stop loving me?

We use the word love *to describe the feelings a man and a woman have for each other, and also to describe the feelings a parent has for a child. But they are not the same kinds of loving. Even though your Mom and I don't love each other anymore, we will both always love you.*

Does Dad still love me even though he doesn't see me every day since you separated?

Dad loves you very much. Maybe you'd like to keep a scrapbook of special things to show him—school projects, artwork, little notes about fun or hard things you've done each day. Next time you two get together why don't you tell him you'd like to plan ways to keep in touch better between visits.

Why can't I live with both of you?

Mom and Dad don't live together anymore. We decided that the best thing would be for you to live with me and see Dad [or Mom] often, at regular times. We are both still your parents and we both want to take good care of you and help you grow up strong and healthy.

If Dad loves me, why doesn't he visit or keep up with his child-support payments?

I know your father loves you. I don't know why he is acting this way. I know you miss him very much. It's okay for you to feel angry. You can talk to me about it if you want to [or to another trusted adult]. In the meantime, even though I can't be your Daddy I am doing my very best to take good care of you.

Did you love the person you were married to before Daddy? What happened?

We did love each other when we decided to get married. But after a while we realized we had many problems. All married people have problems. But even though we tried very hard, we just couldn't work them out. It was a hard decision, but we realized it would be better to stop being married. Now that I'm married to your Daddy, we do have problems and disagreements like everybody else. But we work on them together, and I'm very glad we're married to each other.

Did you love Mom? Why did you get divorced?

I loved your Mom when we decided to get married. But after a while we realized we had many problems. All married people have problems. But even though we tried very hard, we just couldn't work them out. It was a hard decision, but we realized it would be better to stop being married. We both still love you very much.

Did Dad really leave you so he could marry someone else?

Dad did marry someone else right after we got a divorce. The problems we had, and your Dad's decision, are between your Dad and me. It was a very painful time. Now we have a new life. Things are not always easy. Our family is different, but still a family.

or

Ask your father.

Friendship

> I know everything about John and he knows everything about me. We know where the secret places are in each other's house, and that my mother cooks better but his father tells funnier jokes ... We always stick together because I'm good at fights, but John's the only one besides my family who knows that I sleep with my light on at night. He can jump from the high diving board but I know he's afraid of cats ... He saw me cry once and the day he broke his arm I ran home and got his mother for him. ... I know who he really likes and he knows about Mary too. John is my best friend and I'm his.
>
> —Charlotte Zolotow, *My Friend John*

Aristotle considered friendship the school for the training of virtue. In his view, one of the main duties of friends was to help one another grow as human beings; friends were not only to enjoy one another's company, but to be useful to one another and share a common commitment to the good. Today, in the United States, friendship tends to center around shared activities—work, children, recreation. Sometimes the cultural emphasis on being "popular," as David Riesman observed in *The Lonely Crowd*, can actually convey the impression to our children that making friends is more important than our own ideals or commitments. But child-development researchers are increasingly recognizing that children's friends do play an important role in moral and spiritual growth.

Research on children's friendships is comparatively

scarce. Although teachers and child-care workers have long recognized the importance of socialization, for a long time most psychoanalytic theorists emphasized the importance of the mother-child relationship. Peer relations were thought to be little more than a reflection of a child's attempts to gain love and approval from adults. An important exception to this school of thought was the psychiatrist Harry Stack Sullivan, writing in the 1940s, who believed that children's friendships had an impact throughout their lives. He noted that his adult male patients who were very uncomfortable in business or social dealings with other men had lacked opportunities to have close friends, or "chums," before adolescence.

In recent years, though, developmentalists have begun to explore the special role of friendships in children's lives. Much of this new focus is on the unique ways friendships prepare a child for life in adult society. The social psychologist Zick Rubin has pointed out that friendships are an opportunity to learn good and *bad* behavior. Through encounters with friends, children *do* learn how to get along with others. They also learn to reject others ("Treehouse. Keep Out!"), to stereotype them ("Crybaby!"), and to feel ashamed of being different. As in all human relationships, there is a constant tension between their needs for autonomy and affiliation. If a child is such an individual that he makes no friends, he will be lonely. Yet if friendship is the essence of his life, he fails to learn to stand up for himself, to go against the crowd when the crowd is going the wrong way.

During the earliest years, as most parents recognize, children do not have friendships in the sense we think of them. During the *first three years of life* they engage in "parallel play," sitting beside one another with toys but not really interacting. By fourteen months, however, according to a pioneering study of infants' and toddlers' social behavior conducted in the 1930s at a Montreal foundling hospital, toddlers begin to show preferences toward one playmate or another—often because of similarities in developmental level, temperament, and behavioral styles. By the age of two, a child seems to have an idea of what a friend is: a familiar peer she or he can play with. The child who hits, takes toys, or knocks things down is not considered a good friend. Often the child who is most successful socially is the one who unobtrusively slips into the group, rather than asking, "Can I play?" which is almost always answered with an automatic "No." Children's friendships often seem remarkably shallow by adult standards. A three-year-old scolds, "You're not my friend anymore!" after a playmate knocks down her block tower.

By *school age*, children's friendships are based on shared hobbies, liking the same things, knowing one another for a long time, and getting along well. A kindergartner makes friends with anyone who rides his bus or lives nearby. A first-grader likes the child with long blond hair "just like mine." A third-grader chooses friends who enjoy the same hobbies. By school age, children can understand that another person has a point of view. The phrase, "The best way to have a friend is to be one," has meaning now. The child who is outgoing, greets other children, and lets them know what she's interested in ("I play basketball"), asks questions about where they live and what they enjoy doing, and invites them over, makes friends easily at this age. Although individual boys and girls may befriend each other, for the most part friendship groups are single-sex. Because school-age children identify strongly with their particular family and cultural background, according to recent research at Johns Hopkins University, they are unlikely to make friends from other groups unless they have opportunities to work on joint projects together—in the classroom, congregation, or in an after-school activity.

It is not until *preadolescence and the teen years* that friendships begin to include the exchanges of confidences which adults would call real intimacy. Now, as the adolescent works at defining himself in the world beyond home, parents, and school, she shares her deepest secrets with peers in hope of understanding and affirmation. She understands that friendship has its ups and downs, and that commitment to a relationship takes effort. The downside of her need to break away from home and family can show up as a blind conformity to peer-group standards in every area from clothing to music to surprising or mildly delinquent behavior (Halloween pranks, for example). *When an adolescent's whole self is identified with the group—when bonding with peers becomes a means to make up for earlier, unmet needs for love and self-worth, instead of a way to affirm and nurture a fledgling healthy self—then friendship can be the road to trouble.*

As I write this book, a group of affluent high school students in Glen Ridge, New Jersey, have been tried and convicted of repeatedly raping a mentally retarded girl with a broom handle. How could such a thing happen? Obviously, outsiders can only speculate about these teens' backgrounds and motivations. But when teenagers join in mindless or brutal group activity—in a gang, or as part of a cult—they have made a *choice*. They have chosen group validation over individual values and autonomy.

The groundwork for such choices is laid all through the long years of childhood, when we affirm our child's uniqueness and, in the context of family relationships, help her cope with the conflicting demands of self and others. As she asks questions about the challenges of love and friendship, we can help her learn to make healthy, life-giving choices. Day by day we teach her that true love includes struggle, and real friendship does not breed conformity but creativity.

If I'm supposed to love my neighbor, does that include kids who are mean and rotten?

Loving your neighbor doesn't mean feeling all mushy about him. It means appreciating him as a whole person, a human being just like you. And it doesn't mean letting him pick on you, either. You're supposed to "love your neighbor as yourself," not more than yourself. Loving your neighbor means trying to understand that he sees things differently from you. It means that when you get angry at him you tell him your feelings without trying to take revenge. It means caring about him when you get the chance. You might be surprised, even with a mean kid. Sometimes being kind to someone when they don't expect it can be very powerful. Offer an example from your own life of the transformative quality of loving kindness. One boy who got the school nurse for the playground bully when he fell during a soccer game, for instance, was amazed to discover that the bully was a lot nicer to him after that day.

Is it okay to hit back?

I want you to learn to take care of yourself and stand up for yourself. That's important. But hitting isn't the best way to

solve problems between people—it usually only makes every-
body angrier. Let's talk about some other ways to stop another
child from picking on you. Elicit from your child various op-
tions that might be possible responses to another child's
hitting. Role-play ways to defuse an argument (with a younger child, use puppets, dolls, or stuffed animals). Instead of
countering a bully's taunts with more taunts, for example, a
child can learn to stop him in his tracks with a question or
observation: "Why are you acting like this?" or "I guess you
must be pretty mad." Teach your child "tough talking," how
to sound like a menace and scare off the attacker ("Don't
you *dare* hit me or you'll be sorry you ever came to this
school"). Encourage her to *avoid* the class bully and to walk
away before an argument escalates into a fight. Teach him to
distract his attackers by saying something silly or outra-
geous ("Look, Martians are landing on the monkey bars!").

If a child is mean to me, should I tell the teacher?
The first thing to do is to try to handle it yourself. Tell him
in a strong voice, "I don't want you to do that." If the child is
your friend, try to talk about the problem. If the child is some-
one you don't know, then stay out of his way. I certainly don't
want you to get hurt. If the problem keeps happening even af-
ter you've tried your best to handle it yourself, then you may
need to tell the teacher. Encourage your child to express feelings and needs clearly and even forcefully at home, so that
he is confident doing the same with others. Make it clear
that you believe your child has the capacity to speak up for
himself (unless he is at risk of bodily harm). And allow disagreements among siblings to be a learning opportunity by
encouraging them to express feelings (including anger) and
resolve conflicts *without* your interference.

Why is Amy so bossy? Why is Tommy such a brat on the playground?

We can't treat others fairly if we haven't been treated fairly ourselves. People who study children have found that when kids grow up without the love they need—maybe because their parents argue a lot, or they're too busy to spend time with them, or they don't treat them in a respectful way, or they don't teach them how to behave—kids feel awful inside. Then they show it in the way they behave, like attacking other kids.

Tommy acts like a big shot, but inside I think he feels like a very scared little boy.

Why did Ellen give away my secret?

It's fun to share secrets with a friend, but most kids have a hard time keeping a secret. When somebody gives away our secret it almost feels as though they took something private away from us. Maybe next time you have a secret you'd be better off telling a different friend, or writing it down in your journal.

Why doesn't anybody like me?

I guess you had a rotten day today, and it seems as though nobody likes you. Did you have a problem with one friend? Alliances often change during the school years, when children often have a new "best friend" every month. Listen to your child's feelings. Reassure her that she is fun to be with (name some faithful friends if you can). Encourage her to set up a playdate or plan an outing with a child whose company she enjoys.

Why did the other kids make fun of me?

All kids tease sometimes. (School-age children in particular, tend to form "clubs" and taunt nonmembers.) *Some-*

times if you're different—because you wear different clothes, or do well in school, or show your feelings a lot—then kids say you're weird. Maybe they secretly wish they were like you.

Maybe they think the world would be better if we were all the same. But imagine how boring the park would be if there were only one kind of tree. Think how dull dinner would get if you could only eat one kind of food.

For a discussion of how to help a child deal with sexist or racist comments, see pages 140 and 145.

Why didn't I get invited to Susie's party?

When we have a party we need to make choices about whom to invite. We need to have enough room and enough party supplies for all the guests. I guess Susie could only pick her very best friends for this party, just like you did for your birthday. It's not much fun to feel left out, though, is it? Why don't we plan a special outing for you and a friend on that day.

If, on the other hand, your child is conspicuously excluded from a celebration her peers are invited to, the most comforting thing you can do is share your indignation. This is *not* the time to suggest your child brush up on her social skills. She needs empathy. *It certainly is mean to invite everybody except one person! That's terrible. I'm furious Susie would be so rude and inconsiderate.* One mother received a phone call at work from her tearful daughter, who had been jilted by her date for an important party. The mother offered her support in no uncertain terms: "That son of a bitch!" she blurted into the receiver. Later on, said the mother, "I realized it was exactly what she needed to hear."

How come I'm not popular?

What's "popular"?

Sometimes kids are part of an "in" group because they wear the same outfit or have the same haircut or play with the same toys as the other kids in the group. It's not easy to feel like part of the group if you're different. But if you feel comfortable being yourself, you'll find kids whose company you enjoy. This question often comes up with adolescents. Because they still have little cognitive ability to see beyond the present moment, their feelings are likely to be very intense even after one bad day in the school cafeteria.

How am I going to make friends in my new school?

It's a little scary to start out with all new kids. But it's exciting, too. But just like in your old school, your teacher will call out the names of all the kids in the class. You'll do projects together, and meet kids in the cafeteria and on the playground. After school you'll be in activities [Scouts, gymnastics, the Y after-school program], where you'll meet kids who are interested in the same things you are. You're fun to be with and like to do fun things, and before long you'll have new friends you enjoy.

Find out if the school will assign your child a "buddy" for the first day. Help her make friends by encouraging her to reach out. *Would you like to invite a new friend over the first or second week of school so you'll get to know one another better? Or you could invite a couple of classmates to watch a video and have pizza.*

Even if your child says, "I don't care if I don't have any friends," don't be fooled. She will benefit from your encouragement and support. Check with your child's teacher and elicit her cooperation in helping your child connect with compatible classmates.

Can Karen visit us even though she's moving away? Can I still see Karen even though we're moving away?

I know you'll miss Karen. You two had lots of good times together. Now that she will be living far away, you won't get to see her the way you're used to. But you can write letters to each other. And I hope she'll come back to visit. You can be sure to tell her she's always welcome in our home. If your child persists in asking this question despite your clear replies, understand that this is her way of expressing and working through her feelings of loss. Although her repeated questions probably leave you feeling guilty (especially if your family is the one doing the moving), know that she will make the transition more easily with your support.

Exploring Together

Write your family history. Encourage your child to interview family members (parents, grandparents, aunts and uncles) to learn their dates and places of birth, childhood memories (favorite hobbies, embarrassing moments, special food and music). Collect the information in a booklet to keep, or to photocopy for everyone in the family.

Plan special family times. Instead of scheduling activities the family *ought* to do together for educational purposes, set aside one or two times a week for simple celebrations of just being together. Plant seedlings indoors in the spring. Go apple picking. Make a pot of soup. Even if you are not especially proficient, share a hobby: music, basketball, board games. Keep it fun and low-key.

Pass out "caring coupons." Even though your school-age child or adolescent is less likely to cuddle up than she was at an earlier age, she still needs to know that you appreciate her. Set out a pad of stick-on notes in a convenient place, and surprise your child with short love notes or "caring coupons" (worth one hug, one back rub, etc.) on her headboard, mirror, or handlebars. You might wish to encourage one sibling to write notes to another on a day when somebody needs a boost. Who knows? Maybe *you'll* even get one.

The Parent's Path

How did you learn about love? Think back to what your parents told *you* about sex. Did it make sense? Did it sound ridiculous, or disgusting, or hard to believe? Were you ready for their explanations? Or did you learn the "facts of life" from other kids and have a Big Discussion with your parents long after you knew what they were going to explain? What puzzled you about sex as a child? What do you wish your parents had told you? What was your first sexual experience? How did you feel about it at the time? How do you feel about it in retrospect? Remembering your own feelings will help you empathize with your child's.

How's your love life? Do you enjoy sex, or is it disappointing? Do you look forward to it, or would you just as soon go right to sleep? Do you wish you had more opportunity to be romantic? How has your love life changed in recent years? How do you feel about it? How comfortable are you with your own body? How do you feel, as one father put it, about "saying the L-word?" Becoming conscious of your own attitudes and feelings is a good way to recognize the unspoken messages you are sending your child.

Write a "love letter" to your child. Find a quiet time and place and write a one-page letter to your child, telling her some of the qualities you must cherish in her. Mention a few of the memorable moments (funny, touching, exciting) you have shared with her. Now set aside the letter in a safe place and save it for an important occasion—your child's sixteenth birthday, high school graduation, confirmation, bar or bat mitzvah.

Books

FOR PARENTS:
Fromm, Eric. *The Art of Loving.* Bantam, 1970.
Greenspan, Stanley. *First Feelings.* Penguin, 1985.
Warren, Andrea, and Jay Wiedenkeller. *Everybody's Doing It.* Penguin, 1993.

FOR CHILDREN AND PARENTS:
Boegehold, Betty. *Daddy Doesn't Live Here Anymore.* Golden, 1985.
Brown, Margaret Wise. *The Runaway Bunny.* Harper and Row, 1942.
Cleary, Beverly. *Ramona and Her Father, Ramona Forever* (and other titles). Dell and Morrow.
Gormley, Beatrice. *Ellie's Birthstone Ring.* Dutton, 1992.
Munsch, Robert. *Love You Forever.* Firefly Books, 1982.
Paterson, Katherine. *Jacob Have I Loved.* Harper Trophy, 1980.
Williams, Margery. *The Velveteen Rabbit.* Avon, 1922.

•5•

Everyday Ethics

A seven-year-old came home from school one day and told his mother that he had let another child look over his shoulder during a spelling test.

"But cheating is wrong!" his mother said, shocked.

The boy stared at her. "But, Mom," he said in a puzzled tone, "*you* told me I should help other people. He felt awful because he's not good at spelling, and I wanted to help him."

We'd all love to give our children a world in which moral questions have clear-cut answers, the good guys always win, and grown-ups always do the right thing. Instead, day after day we are reminded of life's complexities, and of our own limitations. The platitudes we learned as children—not to mention the "family values" touted in some circles as the solution to all society's problems—are far removed from the realities of life in our households and communities. "I decided to become a Scout leader after I read all the stuff about God, and country, and family in the Scout manual," one mother told me ruefully. "I thought, 'What wonderful ideals!' But working with *real* kids has been a *very* different experience, to say the least."

Children do not learn ethics from ideals or abstract rules. As the research of Lawrence Kohlberg and other theorists of the stages of moral development has shown, moral growth, like all development, happens gradually. It evolves along with our child's maturing abilities to think and as her relationships with family and friends change. Moral theorists have proposed a variety of timetables to mark the development of ethical reasoning, most of them showing how children begin as egocentric creatures, progress to a reciprocal understanding of fairness ("Hey, he got more ice cream than me! It's not *fair!*"), and finally as adults to a sense of abstract moral values.

Yet moral *action* requires more than the development of thinking ability. As several feminist theorists—most notably Carol Gilligan—have pointed out, *caring* is the basis for the development of a true moral sensibility. *Feelings* and *empathy* are essential to morality. Through the most intimate relationships of our lives we learn a way of knowing right from wrong gained through our deep awareness of human connectedness. The ancient Hebrew description of "conscience" is the equivalent of "knowing in one's heart."

In the family context, as a one-year-old offers a half-chewed grape to Mom, as a six-year-old feeds the dog, as an adolescent works at a soup kitchen, each of these children is developing empathy and concern for others. Parents communicate ethics by sharing their genuine concerns and compassion in words and action. Several studies show that the *emotional intensity* mothers showed in teaching children not to hurt others—rather than the skillfulness of their explanations—is the decisive factor in the development of empathy and caring.

> If I speak in the tongues of mortals and of angels, but do not have love, I am a noisy gong or a clanging cymbal. And if I have prophetic powers, and understand all mysteries and all knowledge, and if I have all faith, so as to remove mountains, but do not have love, I am nothing. If I give away all my possessions, and if I hand over my body so that I may boast, but do not have love, I gain nothing.
>
> —1 Corinthians 13:1–4

A life of moral commitment reflects not only a person's ability to reason, but the development of qualities such as determination and courage. These are the stuff of self-esteem. A child can only reach out to others, or take a difficult stand in the face of adversity or temptation, when she feels good about herself and can trust her own experience. Through everyday challenges—building a block tower, getting up from under her two-wheeler after a spill, inviting the playground crybaby to join a kickball game—she is developing the inner strength that used to be called *character* in generations past.

Finally, living ethically demands moral *imagination*. As they grow, children can begin to grapple with moral issues not by oversimplifying them but by being willing to face them in all their concreteness and all their complexity. "I try to be consistent with my kids," mothers frequently tell me, "but life doesn't seem to be consistent." It certainly doesn't. "Being good" is much more than merely being obedient. It is an ongoing *creative* process. "Humans are driven to invent moral criteria," wrote the educational psychologist Jerome Bruner, "as newly hatched turtles move toward water and moths toward light." We need not feel defeated when we are unable to offer simple, straightforward answers to each question our children ask. As we help them struggle with the moral dilemmas of their young lives—as we help them find the delicate balance between justice and caring, and between the demands of reality and our dreams of what might be—we teach them that ethical behavior engages both heart and head. In the Bible, a person's inner moral sense is described in visceral terms—as "heart," "loins," and "bowels." As we encourage a child to listen to himself, to believe in the wisdom of his own thoughts and feelings, to *trust his gut,* we give him much more than a code of behavior. We help him develop an inner compass that will guide him all through life.

Moral Growth

Long before a child can ask ethical questions, the infant's earliest emotions mark the tender beginnings of morality. By the ninth month of life babies express their feelings about the world around them and look for emotional signals from others in order to regulate their own behavior, a phenomenon psychologists call "social referencing." For example, a child in her high chair is likely to check the expression on a caregiver's face before or after letting a piece of banana drop to the kitchen floor.

The *moral emotions*—pride, shame, hurt feelings—begin

to emerge by the middle of the second year of life. The toddler is increasingly aware of her separateness from caregivers, and yet she still looks to them for confirmation that she is "good" or "bad." When she breaks a rule—spilling juice or having an accident on the way to the potty—she hides her face, or goes off to her room to avoid being connected with the "crime."

How does a child develop an inner moral compass? Beginning with the pioneering work of Gordon Allport in the 1940s, and in many studies since, researchers have found that parents who are *authoritative*—as opposed to authoritarian—tend to raise children who get along well with others and have a strong sense of social responsibility. Authoritative parents are loving and supportive, willing to offer explanations for rules, and respectful of a child's point of view. At the same time, they demand mature behavior, set clear limits, and expect children to contribute to the family by doing household chores. In a *supportive but structured environment,* a child has many opportunities to learn everyday ethics. You can help in five important ways.

1. Build your child's self-esteem. As she grows, she begins increasingly to understand that different people have different ways of looking at things, and that her own way is important. When you look carefully at her artwork, notice her special talents on the soccer field, or encourage her to keep a journal, you let her know she's appreciated for the unique person she is.
2. Teach empathy. As early as the age of two, many children will comfort a crying infant, or offer a lollipop to a playmate who has fallen down. Nurture this natural

foundation for morality by helping your child identify his own feelings—sad, happy, worried, scared, lonely, excited. Be sure he has dolls or play figures to play out his feelings in fantasy. If he knows you consider his feelings important, he in turn will care about those of others.

Encourage your child to empathize by asking her to imagine other people's feelings at opportune moments: "How do you think Sarah feels when you hit her?" or "How would *you* feel if your brother ate all *your* Halloween candy?"

One mother noticed her six-year-old and his friends ignoring a younger boy on the playground. She called her son aside and said, "I think that child over there is lonely. Do you know who he reminds me of? Your cousin Charlie, who had such a good time playing with you and the other big kids when we got together last weekend." By helping him connect emotionally with the younger boy's predicament, this mother encouraged her child to behave in a more caring way. "He went over and talked to the boy for a while, then went back to his friends," she recalled later. "It was a step in the right direction."

Contrary to popular belief, empathy doesn't mean *having* the same feeling as another person. Empathy is *understanding* how another person feels. In order to understand, we need to learn to listen.

3. Share responsibility. Having *family meetings* is one of the best ways to introduce your child to ethical decisionmaking. Depending on your family's schedules and style, you can set up regular meetings (weekly or biweekly) or agree that any family member can call a

meeting. Plan regular meetings weekly or monthly in a comfortable room.

Be sure to tell everyone there are three basic rules: Every family member has the right to bring up a topic for discussion, everyone has the right to be listened to attentively, and everyone works together to seek a solution to the problem. As soon as a problem has been brought up by one person, it becomes a *family* problem. Parents and children have equal voices and votes. The majority rules. If, after a week, the agreed-on decision does not prove to work well in practice, plan another meeting. Together the family can brainstorm and come up with a new solution, and take another vote.

4. Show her that her behavior has consequences. Children *construct* early moral knowledge on the basis of social experiences. If I knock down Jamie's block tower, he will hit me or run crying to his mother and go home. If I hit another child, I will be sent to the time-out chair. If I don't follow the rules in soccer, no one will let me join the game.

When we encourage children to recognize their mistakes we often discover that they are surprisingly aware of the rightness or wrongness of their actions. (If your child lies or cheats and you angrily reprimand her, on the other hand, what you teach her is to *cover up*.) One mother told me about the year her seven-year-old discovered his sister's birthday present in the closet (a long-awaited doll) and told her all about it.

"I'm surprised at you," the mother told him. "I thought you were old enough to keep a secret." The boy looked glum, but nothing more was said. That night the mother heard muffled sobs from his room. Soon the boy came out to the living room and sat beside his mother.

"I want to apologize," he said softly. "I'm sorry I told my sister about the doll."

"It wasn't the right thing to do, was it?" she replied.

"No."

"You're forgiven. I love you," she said, stroking his hair. "Try to keep a secret next time, okay?"

The boy hugged her, heaved a sigh, and went back to bed. Later on, his mother told me, she realized their dialogue had followed the age-old form of a confession: the boy had admitted his wrongdoing, and, after encouraging him to mend his ways, she had forgiven him. It seemed to work.

5. Encourage her to "compare notes" with you on moral dilemmas. As we answer questions about ethics, parents naturally help children's ethical education along by engaging in a process known to developmentalists as *scaffolding:* We build on their comments and observations, offering enough supportive guidance to help them onto the next step, in a give-and-take. For example, if your first-grade girl comes home from school complaining that she hates boys because they're all annoying, you're likely to ask why she feels that way. "Because Jason hit me at lunchtime," she answers.

"Oh, I see, so you're angry at Jason." Now you are encouraging her to go from stereotyping to thinking about a specific experience.

"Yeah, and I'm never gonna eat lunch with him again!" She expresses her feelings about Jason, and her plan for revenge.

"Well, nobody likes to get hit. That's one way to avoid it. What else do you think you could do to keep him from hitting you again?" Now perhaps you *role-play* age-appropriate alternatives with your child: A first-grader might try telling Jason she does not like to be hit, walking away from him at times when he seems likely to be aggressive, or asking an adult for help. *By encouraging your child to work on her own ethical questions, rather than handing her answers, you teach her that you value and support her explorations.*

Stages of Moral Reasoning

Children's ability to think through moral questions changes as they grow. A *five-year-old* or younger is likely to approach a dilemma from a self-centered standpoint; young children define right and wrong in terms of their own subjective feelings. For this reason, they may justify taking a toy from another child "because I wanted it." (Yet by the age of five, children around the world have developed the surprisingly sophisticated ability to know the difference between *convention* and *morality*. For example, they know it is inappropriate to use toilet language in front of the teacher—although they delight in doing so with friends at recess—but it is morally *wrong* to steal toys from the classroom.)

By *eight* a child links the "right thing" with parents' and teachers' idea of good behavior. This is the stage the moral theorist Lawrence Kohlberg called "conventional morality," when right and wrong are defined by rules, laws, and the views of authority figures. When the teacher is absent and there is a substitute teacher, it is "okay" to misbehave because the "real" source of authority is missing. Most people never fully outgrow this level (do you find yourself slowing down the minute a police car appears on the road?).

But by *adolescence*, the child's reasoning begins to draw on internalized values and abstract principles. These have little connection with concrete reality: "People shouldn't just pick on each other," a teenager might say. "They should have a good time together." Because ideals are so important during this period, there is little room for lapses by adults, and virtually none for sheer pragmatism. No wonder Mom and Dad are often called hypocrites.

At moments when your child seems to be surprisingly selfish—or annoyingly preachy—recognize that she is probably reflecting her particular stage of moral development. On the other hand, a child's generosity of spirit and ability to grasp contradiction transcend simple categories. Long before children can put moral reasoning into words, they seem to have a sense of right and wrong that grows out of the empathy and care they receive at home.

It's not fair! He got more than me.

Whether the question comes up over potato chips, holiday presents, or storytime with Dad, keep in mind that for young children, "fair" usually means "the same." This is mostly a matter of cognitive development. It will take time and repeated explanations for your child to understand, for example, that four big potato chips are the equivalent of eight small ones. And don't be surprised to hear an older child think that he "should" get more because he's bigger. In a world where he is small and so many are tall, a child tends to understand justice as "getting her share." Rather than scolding her for being "stubborn," affirm her insistence on fairness while encouraging her toward more complex thinking. *I love you both and it's important to me to be fair to both of you. But fair doesn't always mean the same. You have a blue truck and he has a red truck. You play baseball, she plays soccer.*

Why do I have to say thank you for the present from Aunt Sue when I already have one just like it?

Aunt Sue spent time picking it out, and gave her choice a lot of thought. When you say thank you, you are letting her know that you appreciate her caring. And after all, if you already had one just like it she must have had a pretty good idea what kinds of things you enjoy!

Why do I have to clean my room when I'm perfectly happy if it's messy?

We can't vacuum it unless it's clean, and it's not healthy to breathe dust all night.

or

I know you don't enjoy cleaning, but everyone in the family needs to do our part to keep our home nice. Your room is part of our home.

or

I know you're perfectly happy if it's messy. You were per-
fectly happy before you tasted ice cream, too. I gave you your
first ice cream cone because I thought you'd enjoy it. I hope
you'll discover that when your room is neat you can enjoy it
more, too, because your toys and homework will be organized.

Why doesn't Santa Claus come to our house?

Santa Claus only visits children whose families celebrate
Christmas. That is their special holiday, and their special tra-
dition. At our house we celebrate other holidays. Rather than
imply a one-to-one correspondence between different religious celebrations (e.g., "they have Christmas, we have Cha-
nukah"), remind your child of the most important holidays
on your calendar throughout the year. If your child is
young, avoid stating outright, "There is no Santa Claus."
Not only might it lead her to spoil the fun for her friends,
but this reply fails to address the basic issue: that your child
is learning to cope with cultural differences, and—perhaps
for the first time—with her awareness of being part of a religious minority in this country, and perhaps in her classroom. Without pressuring her, let her express her feelings
about being "different." Take this opportunity to involve
your child in some of the customs that are special in your
household.

What's the answer to this homework problem?

Your teacher gives you homework assignments so that you
can work on the material she is teaching in class. I know it's
not always easy, but facing the challenge will help you learn.
If you like, I will sit down with you and listen to the way you

are working through the problem, and maybe together we'll find out why you're getting stuck. But I already went to school and I am not going to do your homework.

Why did the other team cheat?

Everybody wants to win. But unless there's a tie, one team wins and one loses. Some people think they're no good unless they win every time. To them, winning is more important than playing fairly. What do you think that says about what kind of people they are? Give your child a chance to express his moral indignation. Then be sure to tell her you understand her frustration. *It's no fun playing with cheaters. I'm proud of you for being a good sport and playing a good game.*

He did something wrong. Why can't I tell?

You're in charge of making sure you do the right thing. You're not him or his mother. His behavior is their job to worry about. If he hurts you, I want you to tell him to stop. If he doesn't listen, you can go to an adult for help—the teacher, the playground attendant, or whoever is in charge. But unless his behavior is hurting you, then telling is like being a policeman or a tattletale. I know it's frustrating to see him [cheating, disobeying the rules, etc.] when you are trying hard to be good. It's unfair. But I'm proud of you for your good behavior.

Parents Aren't Perfect

No matter how enlightened our answers may be to our child's questions, nothing we say will ever speak as loudly as our everyday actions. Most parents realize this. More than one has told me, "I decide if something's right or wrong by asking myself, 'How would I feel if my child knew?' " Unfortunately, our eagerness to model moral behavior often translates into a daily effort to act like paragons of virtue. No wonder we tend to reward our children for being alert and curious—until they start noticing inconsistencies in *us*.

Yet when we know we've "blown it," we contribute much more to our child's growth by acknowledging the mistake. Let's say you have a bad day at work and arrive home with a throbbing headache. At the dinner table your kids start to tickle each other. You explode: "That's *it!* I've had it! Go to your rooms!"

In the ensuing silence, you are realizing that you probably overreacted. You call the kids back into the kitchen. "I don't like tickling at the table because I want us to have a conversation," you might say. "But I had a bad day today and I'm feeling cranky. I lost my temper, and I'm sorry." By acknowledging your mistake and sharing your own thoughts and feelings, you let your children in on your struggle. You teach them that all through life, people make mistakes and then try to do better.

That's different from paying lip service to morality by saying one thing and blatantly doing another. "I've always told my kids I don't want to hear them make biased remarks," one woman told me. "But lately I've decided if I hear a friend starting to tell me an ethnic joke, I interrupt and say I don't want to hear jokes like that. Usually the response is something like, 'Oh, lighten up.' But if I don't take a stand on this, why am I teaching it to my kids?"

Jason's mother does the hard problems on his homework. Why won't you do mine?

Every parent makes decisions on how to do the best job taking care of his or her child. I want you to do well in school. But I think one of the most important things kids learn from homework is how to face hard challenges. You're brave about doing that, and that's one reason you're such a terrific kid.

Next time you're struggling with a problem, I'd be glad to sit down and help you go over it so we can find out why you're stuck. Listen for a hidden agenda: Are you still at work when your child is working on his assignments? Is he wishing that you would show more interest in his homework? Is he having a hard time with it? Make it clear that you are available and eager to go over difficult problems with him after you get home.

Why is my teacher so mean?

Maybe she had a bad day. This may be your child's way of letting you know he got in trouble in school today. *Did something happen in class that you'd like to tell me about?*

or

She may seem mean to you because she's strict. She wants each child to do their best so that you all learn and grow as much as you can. That's because she cares about you.

or

She does scream a lot, doesn't she? I think that's wrong. I think children have the right to be treated with respect. I wish she used better ways of teaching the class to behave. If your child is doing well in school despite the teacher's behavior, this is an opportunity to let him know he has your support through this tough time. Be sure he realizes that you do not condone abuse by persons in authority (*don't* say, "She's the teacher. It's up to her to do as she likes").

If, on the other hand, your child shows signs of depression or anxiety—sleeplessness, nightmares, morning stomachaches, irritability, loss of appetite, lack of interest in friends and hobbies, or frequent tearfulness—then you probably need to get actively involved.

Set up a meeting with the teacher (you may wish to have your child present). Rather than attacking, try to win her over as an ally. Let her know your child is having difficulties this year. Ask if she has noticed any problems. (She may have a different perspective on your child's classroom behavior, or suggest you have him tested for learning disabilities that are causing him to be disorganized or disruptive.) Tell her you would appreciate her help in helping your child cope with his anxiety. Point out that since she is a very important person in his life, he takes it to heart when she is angry or upset. Name the types of discipline that you find effective with your child at home—time-out or loss of privileges, for example. If your child is present, the three of you may be able to agree on a new approach to discipline that meets your child's needs.

If you don't see improvement after a personal visit to the teacher and your child is in distress, enlist the support of the school psychologist. If, after observing your child in the classroom, he shares your concerns, you may wish to speak to the principle and request a change to another teacher.

Why does Aunt Sarah talk that way about African-Americans [whites, Jews, Latinos, Asians, Catholics]?

You know I believe it's wrong to say bad things about other racial or ethnic groups. That's stereotyping, or making the mistake of thinking everyone who looks a certain way or has a certain name also behaves a certain way. One of the biggest problems is that then, when we feel angry about something, it's very easy to blame it on those "other" people. Aunt Sarah is

*your aunt, and you and I both love her very much. But I think
she may have had a bad experience with one person of that
background and made the mistake of deciding his whole group
is just like that one person.* If a relative makes a biased remark in front of you and your child again, you can offer a
different perspective in a low-key way. "I can understand
that you might feel that way, but let me tell you what my experience is," you might begin. If the behavior continues, you
can simply state that although you enjoy her company very
much, biased remarks are not acceptable in your home.

Why did you lie and tell me there was a Santa Claus?

*When I was a child I liked thinking about Santa Claus and
imagining all the toys he would bring me. I wanted you to enjoy that, too. I'm sorry you feel angry. I think the story of
Santa is one way we have of imagining love and giving. Santa
isn't real, but the idea that you are loved very much certainly
is real.* You might wish to tell your child how the legend of
Santa Claus began. The fourth-century bishop Nicholas of
Myra was celebrated in art and drama for his miracles, especially for saving children from tragedy, and as a giver of
anonymous gifts for the glory of God. His feast day was De-
cember 6, and in many European countries he became
known as Father Christmas. When Dutch settlers brought
the tradition of "Sinterklaas" to New Amsterdam (now New
York), he became Santa Claus.

Although Christian fundamentalists usually refuse to introduce their children to Santa Claus on the grounds that
the myth is idolatrous—and more liberal parents worry that
telling children there is a Santa introduces doubt and mis-
trust into the parent–child relationship—a child's discovery
that Santa isn't real may well serve an important purpose. A

young child needs to experience the joy of receiving, of be-ing provided for. But by school age, it is time to learn a more grown-up lesson, that Christmas is not just about get-ting, and that the secular celebration is not the real story.

Here is the famous reply, published in 1896 in the New York *Sun*, that Francis Church gave to a little girl whose friends had told her there was no Santa:

> Virginia, your little friends are *wrong*, they have been affected by the skepticism of a skeptical age. They do not *believe* except to *see*. They think that nothing can be which is not comprehensible by their little minds. . . .
>
> Yes, Virginia, there is a Santa Claus. . . . Alas, how dreary would be the world if there were no Santa Claus. . . . There would be no childlike faith, then, no poetry, no romance to make tolerable this existence. We should have no enjoyment, except in sense and sight. The Eternal light with which childhood fills the world would be extinguished.

Why do you eat meat? Isn't it wrong to kill animals?

I eat meat because I enjoy it. I don't think people should kill animals unless we plan to use them for food. Animals eat each other, but they don't kill for sport. I am sad to hear that many of the animals we eat are not treated very well by the people who raise them. You can make your own decision about whether to eat meat or not. If your child does not wish to fol-

low the family diet, offer the option of supplementing your regular side dishes with simple protein foods (cheese slices, canned beans). In doing so you are letting your child know you respect his ethical choice.

Why don't you eat meat?

I don't eat meat because it's healthier to eat vegetables, rice, and pasta.

or

I don't eat meat because I don't believe in killing animals for food when there are lots of other delicious, healthy things we can eat. You can make your own decision about whether to eat meat or not. If your child is the family's lone meat-eater, offer simple choices (frozen chicken nuggets, for example). If you feel strongly about not wishing to serve meat in your home, let him know he can eat it in school or order it in restaurants. By allowing him to make a choice, you show respect for his autonomy as an ethical decision-maker.

Did you ever use drugs?

When I was in high school [college] drugs were very popular, and most of us had not learned about how dangerous they are. I did use drugs then. Now that I'm older I realize it was a mistake. I could have hurt my body a lot. I hope you won't ever use drugs. The most famous response to this question in recent years was, without a doubt, then-candidate Bill Clinton's assertion that although he did smoke marijuana, "I didn't inhale." Children, who have difficulty grasping such fine points of ethical behavior, learn more when we are willing to own up to our actions and admit our mistakes.

If alcohol is a drug, why do you use it?

To teach responsible drinking, it is important to take opportunities to answer this question in a low-key way before your child is a teenager. Before offering your own answer, ask if your child has studied about alcohol in school and find out what she already knows. Keep in mind that no matter what you say, your child will notice your patterns of alcohol consumption and is likely to pattern her behavior after yours. *I enjoy having a glass of wine or beer with dinner [or a cocktail at a party]. I never drink a lot. I can have a good time with or without a drink, and there are many things I enjoy that have nothing to do with drinking. I don't use alcohol to cheer myself up. I don't get drunk. I don't drink and drive. I am an adult. When you grow up you may choose to drink alcohol, and I hope you will always do it responsibly. But most kids aren't mature enough to drink, and it is against the law for kids under twenty-one to drink. Drugs like marijuana or crack or cocaine or heroin are against the law for all people. They are dangerous for kids and adults.* If wine or beer are part of your culinary heritage or customs, you may wish to mention this. Ask your child what she would do if a friend offered her something to drink and she didn't know exactly what it was, or invited her to drink alcohol. Get to know your child's friends, and as your child reaches the teen years find out what her friend's parents' attitudes are about teen drinking and what the rules are in their homes. Avoid lecturing your child. Let your child know you want her to be safe and make safe choices, and that drinking alcohol is for adults.

If you do have a problem with alcohol, educate your child. *Many people can drink just a small amount. I can't. I have a sickness that makes it hard for me to stop once I start.*

If you are not staying sober, call Alcoholics Anonymous and encourage your child to join Al-Anon. Your child needs support and, because alcoholism is a pattern in families, she needs to be educated about the fact that she is at risk.

Why are you drinking and driving?

Children who have had substance abuse education in school frequently ask this question when Mom or Dad orders wine or beer with dinner at a restaurant. *I'm having one glass. We're going to be here for about an hour. By that time my body will have used up the alcohol. It won't be affecting me.* Many children are interested in the idea of the "designated driver." *If I'm at a celebration like New Year's Eve or a wedding, where we might be drinking alcohol and need to leave before the effects wear off, then we choose a "designated driver." That person doesn't drink at all, so she or he can drive home safely.*

I know how much I can drink from experience. But kids don't know their limits, and that's why kids shouldn't drink. Make it clear that drinking and driving can cause accidents and even death. (Point out articles in the paper reporting such tragedies as they occur.) By the time your child is a teenager, be sure she knows that even though you do not believe kids should drink alcohol, you have an agreement that she will call you for a ride home rather than drive after drinking or get in a car with a driver who has been drinking. Part of the Students Against Driving Drunk (SADD) contract says parents will pick up their children when called and that there will be "no questions asked" at that time. (For more information, write: Students Against Driving Drunk [SADD], P.O. Box 800, Marlboro, MA 01752.)

How come you can say damn [shit, etc.] and I can't?

Usually bad words are a stupid way to say something you could say more clearly another way. Since I've told you I don't approve of them, I'm going to follow the same rule for myself and not use them either.

or

I save bad words for when I really need them—say, when I stub my toe, or when I hear a politician say something really dumb on television. Most of the time, I don't use them, and I don't think you should most of the time, either.

or

I do use bad words sometimes, but I know when it's not appropriate to use them. It's hard for kids to know the difference, so at this point you're better off not using them at all. As your child reaches school age, you may wish to say that even though you know she sometimes uses certain words with her friends, it is not appropriate to use them with adults or in the classroom.

or

Don't talk about anything you wouldn't want to see on your plate at dinner. One grandfather I talked to said using this rule with kids from kindergarten on up has put an end to bathroom language in his family for three generations.

Why didn't the ref call that foul?

Nobody's perfect. Maybe he didn't see it.

I'm sorry you got hurt. It's frustrating the ref didn't call the foul. I think he made a mistake. Don't be surprised if your child is asking this question because he has heard adults on the sidelines calling the referee names. A question like this one offers you an opportunity to help your child develop a healthier attitude. Let your child know you are not always happy with the referee's calls, but you don't expect anyone to be perfect.

Exploring Together

Create a family scrapbook. In addition to the individual baby books you probably keep, why not try saving materials that represent the collective diversity of the whole family? Collect memorabilia—a baby's bootie, a toddler's curl, a preschooler's first drawing, dried flowers from the back-yard, a paper napkin from a Fourth of July picnic—and put them in a scrapbook, album, or accordion file. As you and your child look through it together on rainy weekend after-noons, holidays, or specially scheduled times, you help him recognize himself as part of an intimate community with shared celebrations and responsibility.

Plan a month of "TV and Talk Nights." Make some pop-corn and get together to watch a family series (reruns of *The Cosby Show* or *Little House on the Prairie,* for example, or *Full House*). When the program is over, ask your child what problem the people in it were working on. Ask her how the different characters saw the issue. Which one did she agree with? How did they work it out? What other choices did they have? Don't be afraid to respond with your own thoughts and feelings, but let your child take the lead.

Talk about everyday moral dilemmas in the news. Whether it's Ann Landers or a hit-and-run accident on a nearby street corner, the newspaper is full of moments when people face moral decisions and their consequences. These stories are far more vivid to a child than dull sermons. When you see a story that grabs your attention, share it with your child. Don't press her to come up with "the moral of the story." Just answer her questions or respond to her comments in a low-key way.

Celebrate everyday triumphs. Most of us are more likely to discipline our children when they do something wrong than to praise them for good ethical decision making. When you are proud of your child's behavior, be sure to let him know. Rather than telling him he is "good," focus on his caring and clear thinking. "You made a good choice," you can say. Or, "I know it wasn't easy to stand up for what you knew was right, and you did it. That's pretty terrific."

The Parent's Path

Play with the "Heinz dilemma." This is the famous moral problem posed by Lawrence Kohlberg to his research subjects.

> A woman is near death. There is only one drug that doctors think might save her, and it was recently discovered by a druggist in the same town. It is expensive to make, and the druggist is charging $2,000—ten times what it cost him to make. Heinz, the sick woman's husband, tries to borrow the money but can only

come up with half of what it cost. He tells the druggist that his wife is dying and asks him to sell it cheaper, or let him pay in installments. But the druggist refuses. Heinz considers breaking into the man's store to steal the drug for his wife.

Should Heinz steal the drug? Why or why not? Or would you have Heinz approach the problem another way? As you experiment with moral reasoning and with the difficulties of reconciling justice and caring, you gain some insight into the challenges that face your child in her exploration of right and wrong.

Take a moral inventory. Write down your strengths and weaknesses. In thinking about weaknesses, focus on personal qualities rather than individual misdeeds (not "I lied to my boss Monday" or "I yelled at my child Thursday" but "I have a hard time facing bad news" or "I lack patience"). What are the consequences of your weaknesses for yourself and others? How do your strengths contribute to those around you? You may wish to share this exercise, which is a version of the Fourth Step of Alcoholics Anonymous and other twelve-step programs, with a trusted friend or confidant.

Books

FOR PARENTS:
Callahan, Sidney. *In Good Conscience: Reason and Emotion in Moral Decision Making.* HarperSanFrancisco, 1991.
Colby, Anne, and William Damon. *Some Do Care.* Free Press, 1992.
Damon, William. *The Moral Child.* Free Press, 1988.
Eisenberg, Nancy. *The Caring Child.* Harvard University Press, 1992.

Gilligan, Carol. *In a Different Voice.* Harvard University Press, 1982.
Kohlberg, Lawrence. *The Psychology of Moral Development.* Harper & Row, 1984.
Lickona, Thomas. *Raising Good Children.* Bantam, 1983.

FOR CHILDREN AND PARENTS:
Banks, Lynne Reid. *The Indian in the Cupboard.* Doubleday, 1981.
Baum, L. Frank. *The Wonderful Wizard of Oz.* Ballantine, 1980.
George, Jean. *Julie of the Wolves.* Harper and Row, 1973.
Kondracki, Linda. *I Always, Always Have Choices.* Revell, 1992.
L'Engle, Madeleine. *Meet the Austins.* Dell, 1981.
O'Dell, Scott. *Island of the Blue Dolphins.* Dell, 1987.
Thomas, Marlo, et al. *Free to Be You and Me.* McGraw-Hill, 1974.

· 6 ·

A Scary World

If Garp could have been granted one vast and
naive wish, it would have been that he could
make the world *safe*. For children and for
grownups. The world struck Garp as unnecessarily perilous for both.

—John Irving

"I'm having such a hard time answering my child's
questions about homeless people," a Manhattan
mother told me, "that I try to cross the street so we don't
have to pass by them."

One man told me about a three-year-old who saw a television news broadcast from Somalia. A network reporter
was talking into the camera, surrounded by emaciated
women and children with swollen bellies. "Why is the one
talking so healthy?" asked the three-year-old simply.

"When my children read the papers, all they see is violence and starvation. When I try to talk to them about ideals
like human brotherhood and peace, they just moan, 'Oh,
Mom,'" said a Seattle mother of two adolescents. "When I
was young I remember being so idealistic. What's wrong
with kids today? How do I share hope?"

Children have always lived in a world filled with loss, pain, and suffering, just as children have always known there were monsters under the bed. They feel safer and secure in the company of loving caregivers. In London during World War II, René Spitz studied two groups of children: those who were sent out of the city to live with sympathetic strangers in the countryside, away from the bombing, and those who remained at home with their parents through the Blitz. Spitz found that despite their exposure to the bombings, the children who remained home with their parents were emotionally healthier at the end of the war than those who had been sheltered in strangers' households.

Sharing hope is far from easy in a frightening and often brutal world. Even trained social workers are so overwhelmed by human need that they are reporting a new syndrome they call "compassion fatigue." But when children ask questions about pain in the wider world—hunger, war, prejudice, AIDS, random violence—we don't help them by avoiding the issues or offering bland reassurances. All questions are *personal.* As a group, children are the hardest hit by poverty. As adults, they will inherit the problems they are asking about now. They need our honesty. They need facts. And they need to learn to respond to their own questions not only with words but *action.*

Put facts in perspective. One reason our children's questions about social, environmental, and political problems can be so intimidating is that they seem to demand "quick takes" on situations that have taken years (even centuries) to develop and are likely to take some time to resolve. Instead of trying to sum up an issue, help your child see it in historical perspective. How did people understand this situation when it started? What have we learned that has changed our approach to it? What do we need to find out? Tell a story. When your child asks about the environment, for example, help her make the connection between knowledge and solutions.

Why is there pollution?

For a long time people didn't realize that many of the machines and chemicals we use every day in the modern world are bad for the environment. Car fumes, industrial wastes, and even household and lawn chemicals have made our air and water less and less healthy. In many countries, including ours, people have persuaded governments to pass laws making it wrong to put chemicals in water and cause pollution in other ways. Now many rivers are actually much cleaner than they were twenty years ago. But more work needs to be done. Give an example of pollution and cleanup efforts in the air or water near your home.

Earth Words

Acid rain. Acid rain is a "soup" made out of chemicals. It is produced when we burn oil and coal to make electricity, and chemicals called oxides of sulfur and nitrogen get released into the air. When these combine with water vapor and sunlight, acid rain forms. It eats away at stone in buildings and makes rivers and lakes unhealthy for fish.

Endangered species. With hunting, poaching, and pollution, and as more people live in wildlife habitats—grasslands, coral reefs, and rain forests— certain animals are disappearing. One of these is the African elephant, hunted by poachers for its ivory tusks. But people are working to save endangered species. For example, it is now illegal to sell ivory, and the penalties for poaching are getting stricter all the time.

Greenhouse effect. When oil and other fossil fuels are burned, carbon dioxide and other gases are released into the atmosphere. These gases act like the glass in a greenhouse. They let the sun's rays pass through, but they trap heat. This makes the world's climate warm up, and changes the weather all over the world. People worry that if the world heats up and ice in mountainous and polar areas melts, the run off may flow into the oceans, raise the water level, and cause floods along the coasts where people live. Also, many parts of the world would get too hot to be farmed.

Ozone layer. If you look at a globe and imagine it to be wrapped in air, that wrapping is the atmosphere. The outer layers of the atmosphere are the stratosphere, which contains the ozone layer, a screen that filters out damaging rays from the sun (ultraviolet rays). Many of the everyday items we use, especially aerosol sprays, contain substances, (chlorofluorocarbons) that damage that protective ozone screen. Without the ozone layer we lose our protection from the sun's ultraviolet radiation, which causes skin cancer. If enough of the radiation reached the earth, it could even destroy life on our planet.

Rain forests. Half of the world's species of plants and animals live in rain forests, even though they only cover 7 percent of the earth's land. The rainforests are being destroyed because the trees are being used for lumber. In your lifetime they will be wiped out unless people who live there find other ways of making a living, and people all over the world stop buying furniture made of teak and mahogany. Scientists and business people are working to find other ways people in these areas can make a living—by raising food, for instance, or plants that can be used to make medicines.

Don't sugarcoat. Children recognize when we are trying to gloss over difficulty and pain because they see things in immediate terms. During the Persian Gulf War, my own son, then six, got daily "news bulletins" from friends with relatives in the armed forces or in Israel. Every afternoon he'd dress up in a soldier costume and march up and down the hallway with a plastic rifle on his shoulder. Clearly, I thought, the media "experts" who were actually advising us not to *tell* children about the war—or to reassure them that it's "very, very far away"—had neglected to take into account the thousands of American children with loved ones in the Middle East, not to mention active imaginations. I watched and waited for an opportunity to help my son share his worries. One night as I tucked him into bed, he looked up at me, brown eyes solemn. "This is the first war of my *whole life*," he said. "I'm worried. Is there anything I can *do?*"

"Well, maybe if children your age learn to get along better with one another than we grown-ups do," I offered, "you won't have wars like we do now."

"Oh, Mom," he scoffed. "You should *see* the fights on the playground!"

Kids know what's real. To deny reality by trying to shelter them (what one father called the "changing the subject approach" to hard questions) is to damage our own credibility and to cheat them of the opportunity to learn, to grow, and to begin to cope with troubling issues.

Why is there war?

Human beings have always fought wars. I know grown-ups at school and home tell you not to fight. It must be hard to understand why we end up fighting ourselves. Wars happen when countries who have differences give up trying to talk about their disagreements and find solutions, and instead just decide to use force. The United Nations and other groups try to resolve differences peacefully.

Will a nuclear bomb blow up the world?

A nuclear bomb would not do that. It would kill a lot of people and animals and plants. That's why people and governments are working on learning other ways to work out problems, and making agreements to slow down on making bombs. Don't "explain" random violence, epidemics, or natural disasters. As I write this book, floods are devastating Missouri, and the papers report that many believe these were "caused" by the legalization of gambling in that state. For years now people have sought to attribute the AIDS epidemic to divine retribution against homosexuals. Even though it may seen comforting to give a "reason" for a painful event or situation, in the long run we are more honest and more helpful if we allow our children to recognize that not all pain in life can be explained. It just *is*. As human beings, sometimes the best we can do is mourn together and pick up the pieces.

Why did that flood happen?

That flood happened because there was a very big storm and the wind blew water up into our streets. It was very unusual.

or

We often get floods in our part of the country. That's why we build houses designed to be safe. Unfortunately, it doesn't always work.

Why are bad people bad?

Most of us are a mixture of good and bad. Hardly anybody is all good or all bad all the time. We all have choices about what kind of people we want to be. Not everybody knows that, though. Sometimes people think life will be a lot easier if they choose to do wrong things, like a schoolchild who thinks it's easier to cheat on a test instead of learning the lesson. In the long run, it doesn't usually turn out that way.

Some people turn out bad—or treat other people badly— because they don't feel very good about themselves, because they think the world is a bad place and nobody cares what they do. Maybe they didn't feel very loved when they were kids. Maybe their parents were too busy for them or hurt them. But as you grow up, I hope you will know that you can always find

people who do care about you, even when you're feeling that
everything is awful.

Why did that person get shot on the street?

It was a terrible, tragic crime. I wish I knew why it hap-
pened. The person who did it didn't see or care about the pain
he caused. What a waste. I feel angry and very sad. Reassure
your child that you take good care of her and that you are
teaching her to take care of herself. With a child of nine or
ten, you may wish to point out that random acts of violence
seem to occur more often in societies such as ours, with a
weak social fabric and ready access to handguns.

What's AIDS?

AIDS is a sickness. The initials stand for "acquired immune
deficiency syndrome." "Acquired" means you don't get AIDS
by inheriting it, the way you do brown eyes or red hair. You
"catch" the virus from another person's body fluids. "Immune
deficiency" means the body doesn't have the strength to fight
sicknesses and germs the way it usually does. A "syndrome" is
a collection of sicknesses. In AIDS these take over when the
body can't fight anymore—tiredness, chills, fever, diarrhea,
weight loss, and purple or black tumors.

AIDS is the last stage of infection with HIV (the human
immunodeficiency virus). People who are first infected with
HIV don't show symptoms for years. If a person knows he has
HIV he can help himself by eating well, exercising, and getting
good medical care so that the spread of the virus through his
body gets slowed down. Even though people with HIV may not
have symptoms, they can still spread the disease.

When people with HIV get weaker—usually five to eight

years after they get HIV—they are in the next stage, AIDS-related complex (ARC).

When people with HIV get very weak, then they are diagnosed with AIDS. Right now most people with AIDS live a year or longer. Doctors are working hard to find new ways to treat this sickness.

How do people get AIDS?

People get AIDS by contact with the body fluids of someone who has the HIV virus. This usually happens by having sex, sharing hypodermic needles, or contacting blood. (If a woman has HIV and gets pregnant, she can pass it on to her fetus.) You don't get AIDS by playing soccer on the playground, sitting together in the classroom, sharing a toilet seat, or hugging. For a description of safer sex, see page 86.

Am I going to get AIDS?

If you are careful about sexual contact and always follow the rules for safer sex, you probably won't get AIDS. The only way to be sure not to get AIDS is to avoid exchanging body fluids with another person. Making love is something to save for someone you know very well, feel very close to, who cares about you. It is a kind of sharing that is very deep and touches our strongest feelings. I know a lot of teenagers do have sex, but I think you will be happier—and I know you will be safer—if you can wait until you are older. For a description of safer sex, see page 86.

People used to get the virus from blood transfusions, but our blood supply is now screened and it seems to be safe.

Will a burglar break in?

We keep our doors and windows locked when we need to, so that the only people who come to our house are people we want to see. Once in a while a burglar does break into a house or apartment—usually after checking to be sure nobody is home. If that happens, it's very upsetting because nobody likes to think of a stranger taking their things. But it is very unusual for a burglar to break in when somebody is home.

If a burglar ever did break in, we would try to avoid letting him know we were home and call the police right away. Give your child a chance to practice calling the police. Be sure he knows the emergency number, and can clearly state your address and phone number into the receiver.

Could a kid knife me at school?

Sadly, as violence in schools becomes increasingly common, parents need to take this question seriously.

Some of the students in your school seem to think they need to use weapons in order to feel important. That's wrong. Mention it if your school is now checking students as they arrive every day. *One thing you can do to protect yourself is make sure you stay in places where there are lots of other kids and adults around. Avoid kids you know are troublemakers. If you see another child being attacked, get an adult right away.*

Get mad. "When I was a child my father's boss came to our house one day," an African-American mother of three told me. "He called my father Bill, even though his name was William, and my father called *him* Mister Smith. My father never said a word about it, but the message was clear. We blacks were supposed to know our place—and stay there." Sometimes the most helpful—and compassionate— thing we can do for our child is to share our outrage. According to research by the California theologian Joanna

Rogers Macy (who was studying teen-parent dialogue on nuclear war), when parents avoid difficult subjects or show little emotion about them, children tend to interpret our silence as a *lack of caring* about the issues, and they feel alone with their worries. Expressing your dissatisfaction with the status quo is one way to empower your children to trust their own inner sense of justice.

"I heard two men talking during our soccer game," my daughter, then five, told me during her first year on a team. "They were laughing because we were tying our shoes when we were out on the field. They said *boys* would just play and not worry about their shoes." She looked glum. "They said in a few years we would be taking out *mirrors* and fixing our makeup during a game!"

I had overheard the men talking, not realizing she had been within earshot. "What did *you* think about what they said?" I asked.

"Stupid!"

"Yeah, it *was* stupid. You girls play hard, don't you?"

"Yeah."

"You know what you call the kind of thing those men said?"

"What?"

"*Sexist*. That's when people say we act a certain way— usually a silly way—just because we're girls or women."

I wish my daughter were growing up in a world without sexism. She isn't. Since she was born, I've made it a point to supply her with toy trucks as well as dolls, science kits along with poetry books. She has read biographies of Sojourner Truth, Laura Ingalls Wilder, and Marie Curie. But everyday life is already beginning to teach her that the struggle is far from over. In the years ahead she will come to define sexism on the basis of her own experience, and in the process she will need to share more indignation.

Whether you are answering questions about discrimination, abuse, or corruption, by showing your feelings you share your values.

What's sexism?

Sexism is thinking that people have fewer rights because they are female. Men and women are different in some ways. But when women are not hired for certain jobs, or get paid less than men for the same work, or when girls are not called on in class or don't have the chance to take part in certain programs, that's sexism. Things have gotten better in a lot of ways. When Mommy was a child girls didn't play on soccer teams or in Little League. There were no women on the Supreme Court or in Congress. Now lots of countries even have women prime ministers. But work still needs to be done.

What's abortion?

Abortion is ending a pregnancy. The embryo or fetus is taken out of the pregnant woman.

Abortion is legal in the United States, but people have strong disagreements about it. Some think it is the same as murder. Others think that it is part of a woman's right to control her own body. Others think abortion is wrong but needed or there would be many unwanted babies born who would not be cared for. You will probably wish to share your own thoughts and opinions in a low-key way, but point out that this is a complex issue. If your child continues to ask about it, help her or him see the larger picture. *Your question leads to other questions. People disagree about whether an embryo*

or fetus is the same as a baby, or at what point in the preg-
nancy it becomes a baby. And since many of the women who
have abortions are poor, if abortion was illegal or their govern-
ment health program didn't pay for it, what would happen?

What's a battered woman?

Sometimes when a man doesn't feel very strong or impor-
tant, he gets very angry and picks on his wife or girlfriend. If
he hits her or hurts her, that is battering her. It's wrong.

Sometimes if a woman was not treated well when she was
growing up, she may not realize that she deserves to be treated
much better than that. She may think she can't get help. But
there are organizations and shelters for battered women, and
lots of people want very much to help them know they can be
safe, strong, and happy.

What's child abuse?

Rather than offering your child all the information in this
answer, ask him where he's heard about child abuse and
invite him to share with you what he knows about it. Listen
carefully and then offer just enough additional information—a sentence or two—to clarify what he has told you
and provide reassurance. By not overwhelming him, you
leave the door open for further questions in the days and
months to come. *Child abuse is hurting a child on purpose.*
It can mean hitting or kicking the child, or not giving him the
care he needs. Even if a child misbehaves, he deserves to be
cared for. Most parents love their children very much and
want to take good care of them. All parents yell at kids some-
times, but that's not child abuse.

One kind of abuse that might not hurt is sexual abuse. That

means touching a child's private parts, or asking the child to
touch the adult, or doing other things with a child's body that
only grown-ups should do with each other. Even though that
might even feel good to a child sometimes, it's wrong for adults
to do it. It's also wrong for a grown-up to try to make a child
promise to keep any kind of touching a secret, or to try to scare
him or her into not telling.

(If a child is abused by a parent, teacher, babysitter, priest,
minister, or rabbi, he can tell a teacher or other adult who
can get help.) *No matter how bad or scared a child feels, he*
can always talk to a grown-up who cares. You can always talk
to me.

**Why did that government person quit? What's corrup-
tion?**

Corruption means spoiling. When a leader we are supposed
to be able to trust does something wrong in his job—like using
taxpayers' money for himself, or hiring his relatives for gov-
ernment jobs—then that's corruption. It's wrong, because peo-
ple in the government are supposed to serve the public, who
elects them and pays them.

What's the Holocaust?

The Holocaust was the killing of millions of people by the
Nazis, a hate group led by Adolf Hitler in Germany, during
World War II. Six million Jewish men, women, and children
were killed in concentration camps. Millions of Roman Cath-
olics and gypsies were also killed. The Germans wanted to
wipe these people off the earth. It was one of the most horrify-
ing things human beings have ever done, and it is hard for me
to talk about it with you.

There have been other holocausts through history. When

one group of people decides that another group is to blame for all their problems, sometimes they think the only solution is to try to kill everybody who belongs to that group. People who survived the Holocaust want us to remember that it happened so that we will never let this kind of horror happen again.

Why are people rioting and looting?

They are very angry about the way they are treated in our city [or country] and they believe this is the only way they can get their feelings heard. I understand why they're so angry. I do think they've been treated badly. But I think there are better ways to make change, by working through the government and community groups.

What's racism?

Racism is treating another person, or group of people, differently because of the color of their skin. We all notice differences between people, but when we use our power to treat people badly because they're different, that's racism. That includes not letting them buy or rent a house, not hiring them for a job, or calling them bad names.

What's anti-Semitism?

Anti-Semitism is disliking people or treating them badly because they are Jewish.

Why is that man's skin dirty?

His skin isn't dirty. That's the color of it. It's darker than yours because that was the color of his mother and father's skin. His ancestors came from Africa, and there—and in most other parts of the world—people's skin is a deeper color than ours. He is an African-American.

Why are that person's eyes slanted?

They are shaped differently from ours because he is Asian or his ancestors were Asian. That is the way people's eyes look in Asia. Help your child find Asia on a map or globe. Avoid denying racial differences; by pretending to be "color-blind," you imply to your child that there is something wrong with diversity. Instead, acknowledge your child's observation and explain it in a matter-of-fact way.

I wish my skin was white. Why isn't it?

Your skin is the color of Mommy's and Daddy's. It's beautiful. Help your child recognize her skin as the color of precious substances—coffee, chocolate, bronze, copper, autumn leaves. Be sure she has dark-skinned dolls to play with. Share stories and folk tales about beautiful princesses with dark skin. One mother told her daughter, "Your skin must be a beautiful color. Look at all the white people who stay out in the sun all summer trying to get a tan!"

In the late 1930s and early 1940s, Kenneth and Mamie Clark documented the impact of negative racial images on African-American children by offering them a choice between black and white dolls. Sixty-seven percent of the black children chose to play with white dolls. In 1985 clinical psychologists Derek S. Hopson and Darlene Powell-Hopson found that 65 percent of black preschoolers *still* chose white dolls. The psychologists then read a story in which two black children were depicted as the smartest and best students in their class. They talked about the black dolls, calling them "pretty," "nice," "handsome," and "good." They asked the children to repeat these adjectives. After the session, the kids showed a big change of heart: Now 68 percent of the black children chose to play with the black doll.

Why did that person call us niggers [kikes, spics, wops, or another racial epithet]?

People who call other people bad names usually don't like themselves very much. By putting others down they try to feel more powerful.

- Help your child role-play what she will do if the same thing happens again. She can learn to say, "Please stop calling me that name. I don't like it." She can also get help from a classmate or teacher.
- Let her know that it's okay to be angry, that she is lovable and precious to you, and that you will help her learn how to deal with racism.
- If you hear someone making a biased remark, practice polite dissent. Ask, "Why do you think that?" or "Why do you feel that way?" After allowing the person to express himself, share some of your own thoughts.
- Make it clear to your children that biased language is not allowed in your home. One mother told her children these were "hate words."

Get involved. Tragedy and pain in the newspapers and on the streets will be less overwhelming to your child if your family can focus on a particular issue and work toward change. Help your child understand her questions as part of an ongoing search for solutions. (If your child likes Nancy Drew or the Hardy Boys, you might draw an analogy to detective work.) See "Exploring Together" (page 147) for a plan of action.

Why is that person lying on the sidewalk?
That person probably doesn't have a home to live in. He's homeless.

What's homeless?
Homeless people don't have a house or apartment to live in. They have no place to sleep at night, and no place to cook their meals. Sometimes they stay in a shelter, where they can eat and wash up. But there aren't enough shelters for everybody who needs them. So some people live in cars, parks, abandoned buildings, or on the sidewalk. I hope it won't always be this way. (For questions about poverty and wealth, turn to pages 162 and 166.)

What happened to his home?
Maybe he doesn't earn enough money to pay the rent or the mortgage. Maybe he doesn't have a job. There might have been a fire in his home and he didn't have insurance to pay for another one. Maybe he is too sick in his body or his mind to take care of himself or a home. Maybe he is using all his money to pay for alcohol or drugs.

Why does he look so awful?
Your child may not explicitly ask this question, but you may notice that he is clingy or anxious as you walk by a homeless person. *That person looks messy because he doesn't have a place to wash his face or brush his hair or shave. He might be sick. I don't think he wants to hurt us at all, but I can understand why you're afraid. It's okay to hold my hand if you'd like.*

Can we give him money?

We do give money to organizations that give homeless people a place to live, or food, or job training. That way we're sure the money is being used in ways that will really help.

Are we going to be homeless?

We have a place to live and jobs that pay enough so that we can afford the things we need. We may not always have everything you might want or your friends have, and you may hear us worrying about money sometimes, but we aren't going to be homeless.

Exploring Together

Your family in history. When a child recognizes himself as part of a long line of people who have taken part in the events and struggles of their times, he learns that he can make history. Invite your child to interview older people—grandparents, aunts and uncles, neighbors—about their own lives. What were the headlines when they were ten years old? What community organizations or groups did they join? Did they fight in a war, or volunteer on the home front? How did the Depression, or the Vietnam War, affect their daily lives? Did a political candidate or government official ever visit their neighborhood or town? Whom did they vote for the first time?

A nine- or ten-year-old may wish to collect the information and put together a short work of local history, with illustrations or old photos from the public library or local historical society. He can take it to school or donate it to the

children's section of the public library to share with other
kids.

Breakfast with the newspaper. When my kids were tiny
and mornings were a rush of feedings and changings, I
sorely missed mornings with *The New York Times.* What a
joy it was, only a few years later, to discover they were old
enough to be interested in sharing the events of the day.
Look over the front page together. Point out major happen-
ings (stories about royalty, sports heroes, and science seem
to be especially popular, but follow your child's interest).
Your child may wish to share his news as part of "show and
tell" at school, or collect important clippings in a scrapbook.

"Adopt" an issue.

1. Call a family meeting. Say that you have noticed that
   family members are concerned about problems facing
   people today—in your neighborhood, your town, this
   country, the world. Suggest that you make a plan to
   work together as a family to try to put your caring
   into action.
2. Help the group focus on one issue that seems to be on
   everyone's minds. Invite each member to bring up a
   problem and explain his or her personal interest in it.
   Take a vote. (Keep a record of all the issues brought up
   so that no one feels ignored; agree on a six-month "re-
   view" to see if the family would like to continue working on the issue you've voted on, or make a change.)
3. Devise a plan to work on the issue you've chosen. Try
   to include participation on local, national, and global

levels. For example, if the issue that seems to concern your family most is hunger, your local involvement might be volunteering at a nearby soup kitchen or participating in a food drive. Your family can work on the national level by joining Bread for the World, the educational organization that lobbies on behalf of hunger issues. You can make a difference internationally by contributing to Save the Children or another organization that offers an opportunity to sponsor a child and communicate with him or her by mail.

4. Have regular meetings to exchange information, share reactions to your project, and evaluate your efforts.

Share stories. Barraged by frightening news reports and street scenes, our children need hope. Traditionally, visions of a better world, and of triumph over hard times, have been passed down from one generation to the next through stories. Family anecdotes, biographies, folk tales, and sacred stories speak to our hearts and minds of challenges faced and victories won. They nurture the wonder and connectedness that empower us to work toward change. Visit the public library and help your child choose biographies of pioneers, patriots, and sports figures. Check the "Books" section below for illustrated collections of folk tales and myths.

The Parent's Path

How were social issues dealt with when you were growing up? Can you remember wondering about, or asking your parents to explain, a particular problem or news event? What response did you get? Was it satisfying? Overwhelming? Were your parents involved in the community? Did they encourage your involvement?

Pray the news. "More trouble in Bosnia." "Northern Ireland again." "Another murder in New York City." It's no surprise we tend to shut out the pain we read about in the morning paper. Day after day it seems to have no end. We feel helpless. Yet by being *more* attentive to the issues you read about, you can gain courage and hope for talks and action with your child. Set aside fifteen minutes one morning or evening a week to sit down with the front page of the day's paper. After reading each article (including the ones you might ordinarily gloss over), take a few moments of silence, or say a simple prayer ("For these I pray"). Conclude by remembering all those around the globe who are "praying the news" with you on this day.

Books

FOR PARENTS:

Bellah, Robert, et al. *Habits of the Heart.* University of California Press, 1985.

Coles, Robert. *Children of Crisis* (5 vols.). Atlantic–Little, Brown, 1967, 1972, 1978. Also, *The Political Life of Children.* Atlantic Monthly Press, 1986.

Edelman, Marian Wright. *The Measure of Our Success.* Beacon, 1992.

Garber, Stephen W., et al. *Monsters Under the Bed and Other Childhood Fears.* Villard, 1993.

McGinnis, Kathleen and James. *Parenting for Peace and Justice: Ten Years Later.* Orbis, 1990.

McGinnis, James. *Helping Families Care.* Meyer Stone, 1989.

Wiesel, Elie. *Night.* Bantam, 1986.

FOR CHILDREN AND PARENTS:

Anno, Mitsumasa. *Anno's Journey.* Philomel, 1978.

Boorstin, Daniel J. *The Landmark History of the American People.* Random House, 1987.

Brink, Carol Ryrie. *Caddie Woodlawn.* Macmillan, 1935.

Buntin, Eve. *How Many Days to America.* Clarion, 1988.

D'Aulaire's Book of Greek Myths. Doubleday, 1962.

Forbes, Esther. *Johnny Tremain.* Dell, 1943.

Grahame, Kenneth. *The Reluctant Dragon.* Holiday House, 1953.

Hamilton, Virginia. *The People Could Fly: American Black Folktales.* Knopf, 1985.

Jaffrey, Madhur. *Seasons of Splendor.* Puffin, 1985.

Mayo, Gretchen Will. *Earthmaker's Tales.* Walker and Company, 1989.

Near, Holly. *The Great Peace March.* Henry Holt, 1993.

O'Dell, Scott. *Sarah Bishop.* Houghton Mifflin, 1980.

Qunsey, Mary Beth. *Why Does That Man Have Such a Big Nose?* Parenting Press, 1986.

· 7 ·

Money

They can eat five bowls of cereal in one sitting. They leave the front door open when the heat is on. They ask for countless things in a single day. At times we wonder, "Don't they have any idea how much everything costs?"

Probably not. And yet, unless we talk to them about money, how can we expect otherwise? "At our house, *nobody* is materialistic," one mother told me, grinning ironically, as we watched her five-year-old daughter pick out a teenage doll's evening gown and tiara from a vinyl suitcase stuffed with tiny outfits. "Barbie needs every accessory she can get," the little girl told us matter-of-factly as she slipped the doll's long legs into the sequined dress. "Otherwise she won't be complete!"

Many of the parents in my workshops talk about the challenges of taking a spiritual approach to childrearing in a culture in which wholeness is all too easily understood as having every accessory we can get. We all joke that our children cost us much more than we ever imagined, and as we field countless requests for jeans, sweaters, toys, video games, books, and tapes, we find ourselves wondering whatever happened to the simple life. To be "spiritual" about money sounds like it might mean forcing our kids to give up computer games, play with cornhusk dolls, and wear hand-me-downs. "I want my kids to know there's more to life than money," parents tell me.

Ironically, the most effective way to help children put money in perspective is to talk *more* about it. To offer a child platitudes, or simplistic behavior modification techniques, is bound to be ineffective and naive. Our experiences with money shape us at the core, from the time we are very young. The way we get, spend, and save money speaks volumes about the values we hold dear. If you want to examine your spiritual life, someone told me once, look in your checkbook.

Fairy-tale wisdom has it that happiness and money go hand in hand. The hero or heroine starts out poor but virtuous, and ends up rich and happy. Often parents soft-pedal the materialism in this message. "You don't have to have money to be happy," we say apologetically as the poor heroine rides off to the king's castle, or the orphan becomes a prince. I've seen modern retellings of the tales that have the protagonist "rich with happiness and children" instead of the traditional gold.

One fairy-tale heroine who is an exception—poor but joyous—is Hans Christian Andersen's *The Little Match Girl*, and her story illustrates the dangers of separating happiness and money. On a cold New Year's Eve the barefoot girl is selling matches in the street. She lights one match after another to warm her numb fingers, and in the bright clear flame she sees visions of loveliness: a big stove with a splendid fire, a roast goose stuffed with apples and prunes, a Christmas tree shining with thousands of lighted candles.

The fourth time the girl lights a match, she sees her grand-mother, the only person who has ever been kind to her. She lights a whole bundle of matches, hoping to hold on to the vision until finally the grandmother "lifted the little girl up in her arms, and they soared in a halo of light and joy, far, far above the earth, where there was no more cold, no hun-ger, and no pain—for they were with God."

In the morning the little girl is found dead on the street corner, but the storyteller insists that this is a happy ending. "Nobody knew what beautiful visions she had seen," he writes, "nor in what a halo she had entered with her grand-mother upon the glories of the New Year."

I haven't yet met a child who is satisfied with the little match girl's visions or halo. "The girl *died?*" they ask, stunned. "What about the happy ending?"

No wonder the traditional wisdom of fairy tales appeals to kids. If you've ever lost a job, struggled to balance the family budget, or checked the mailbox for child-support payments, you know that heavenly visions of happiness are not enough. Money is part of happy-ever-after endings be-cause body and soul are inseparable.

The word *wealth* relates to *wellness.* Not money itself, but the *love* of money is "a root of all kinds of evil," we read in 1 Timothy 6:10, a verse that is often misquoted. When we encourage our children to take money seriously, when we seize opportunities to teach them that our possessions are gifts, we help them connect getting and spending with their deepest selves. Yet more often than not, the only les-sons our children get about money matters at home are un-spoken ones. "We are tattooed by our families' financial ups and downs," wrote Nora Gallagher in *Family Therapy Networker* (March/April 1992).

The taboo against speaking about money in families is usually so strong that to ask about it is to seem rude, or worse, greedy. We collude in keeping money's role in our lives a secret and its power over and among us intact.... What many people get from their families instead of instruction is modeling. Modeling means that information about money is mixed up with emotional baggage. Fear, envy, shame, guilt are all attached to money like price tags and they cloud attempts people make to deal with money once they have it.

Today money is as infrequently discussed, and yet as powerful in its hold over us, as sex was in our grandparents' time. When we show our children that we get and spend in proportion to our real needs and resources, and when we talk about family money decisions on a regular basis—how we're saving for their education and for hard times, our housing costs, car, insurance, and vacation plans—we teach our children the way they learn: concretely.

Only through experience does a child learn that saving up for a prized stamp collection or tennis racquet can be more deeply satisfying than using the same sum for the sneakers "everybody else has." Day by day, as children lose coins in gum machines, trade baseball cards, and raise money to save the rain forest, they learn the power and limitations of money. They learn, as Jacob Needleman has pointed out in *Money and the Meaning of Life*, that money *can* buy happiness—but not *all* happiness.

> "... when we seek unnecessary things, we have difficulty in finding that which is indispensable."
> —Maimonides, *Guide for the Perplexed*

Money Learning: A Developmental Guide

No wonder children have trouble understanding how money works. Gone, along with the ticker tape, are those time-honored economic institutions of childhood, the lemonade stand and passbook savings account. Even coins are perplexing: If the nickel and penny are larger than the dime, why are they worth less? Nonetheless, long before children are capable of doing simple arithmetic—like summing up three weeks' worth of allowance—they are beginning to develop *attitudes* toward money. From our spending habits and remarks, they pick up on our feelings about it. They have possessions of their own, learn to take care of them properly, and discover that some last longer than others. In the process they learn *stewardship*, an old-fashioned word for the care and wise use of all our gifts.

Toddlers. As your child struggles with the idea that the world has rules—about eating, playing, and using the potty—your gentle encouragement and clear limit-setting help her develop the self-control and autonomy that will be the basis for all responsible decision making.

The toddler can begin to learn to keep toys in a special place, keep track of small vehicles and figures, and take good care of them. Do not expect her to share all her play-things. Instead, set aside a few "special toys" and a larger number of "sharing toys." Before a playmate comes to visit, help your child choose her favorite two or three possessions and put them away on a high shelf; she does not have to share these. In all these ways she is beginning to learn that she can make choices about her possessions, and that in making choices she needs to take into account both her own wishes and the needs of others.

Preschoolers. Most of us indulge in some magical thinking about money all through life (who hasn't bought a lottery ticket?), but in the preschooler this is the predominant feature of the child's thought. "It's *mine,*" she says, seeing an appealing toy. Why? "I want it." And after all, when grown-ups want money don't they go to the bank, where the automated teller machine gives it away? Actually, the preschooler's egocentricity is a healthy sign. She feels loved and deserving. The world is her oyster.

Although three- and four-year-olds can rarely add up dollars and cents, they are soaking up attitudes and values about money from caregivers and the media. Take a few moments to ask yourself, What is our family's routine teaching our child about money?

- Do you work so much overtime that you rarely enjoy unstructured hours at home to do things like playing Candyland or baking cookies? By showing children about the trade-offs you make between time and money, you teach a very early lesson about what really matters to you. "My father turned down a promotion because he would have had to spend a lot more time at the office away from the family," recalled one man, now a father of two. "It was a very clear message about where his values were, and thirty years later I've never forgotten it."

- Do you offer your child treats and rewards as a substitute for your presence more often than you'd like? We all succumb to the occasional souvenir or present after an out-of-town trip or a late night at the office, but if this becomes a pattern you may need to stop and wonder, "Why am I buying my child this gift? Does she need it, or would *time* with me mean more to her?"
- Does your family enjoy priceless pleasures and satisfactions—hikes, trips to the public library, or picnics in the park—or does fun together always carry a price tag?

When your preschooler asks about money, you'll notice that her questions are closely tied to her personal interests and needs. Try to keep your answers as simple and close to her concrete experience as possible.

Why is this toy so expensive?

Even though the plastic it's made out of doesn't cost very much, the company that makes the toy spends a lot on television commercials trying to get kids excited about buying it. The cost of those commercials is part of the price.

Mommy, why do you have to go to work?

I work because I enjoy what I do, I think it's worth doing, and we need the money.

Is being a garbageman [cowboy, firefighter, nurse] a good job?
Any job is a good job if it's honest work. To decide on a good job for you, you need to think about what you're good at, what you really enjoy doing, and what needs to be done.

The school years. A six- or seven-year-old is delighted to visit the five-and-ten and spend an hour looking over the merchandise, although she may end up buying nothing more than pipe cleaners or a pencil sharpener. She appreciates getting an allowance, earning extra money for chores, and endlessly calculating how long it will take her to save up for a special ball or magic ring.

Because school-age children are such enthusiastic comparative shoppers, this is a good time to help them reason out the consequences of their choices. There is nothing awful about wanting to buy the "in" sneakers; unless taken to extremes, this shows a healthy wish to be part of the peer group. But why not encourage a child to think about choosing a less expensive pair and imagine what she could buy with the difference—art supplies, sports equipment, a game? (Also help your child to find other ways to be accepted by peers—learning a popular sport or joining a new school activity.)

Share some of your own financial decision making. Plan a family meeting to get ideas from everybody on ways to save money. If everyone makes an effort to turn off lights when leaving a room, for example, you will see a drop in the electricity bill. Use the difference for a family outing to an ice-cream parlor or game center.

Saving comes naturally to seven- and eight-year-olds, who stack their rooms with collections of all kinds—

baseball cards, stamps, coins, and jewelry. As they accumulate and trade their treasures, they learn that they can be active agents in their school-age financial world. It is important, though not always easy, to recognize that they learn by setting their own priorities. One father told me that his son received some money for his birthday and asked to go to the baseball card store. "Wouldn't you like to save some of that money for something really *special?*" his father suggested.

The boy looked puzzled. "Not really, Dad," he replied. "Baseball cards are very important to me right now."

School-age children explore the value of money the way they explore everything else—by counting it out, adding it up, trading it, and sharing it with special friends. If they like another child, they are likely to show it with a gift of a toy or even a dollar. Rather than accusing them of trying to buy friendship, acknowledge the generous impulse and point out that there are other, longer-lasting ways to be nice—by being a good friend, sticking up for a buddy on the playground, planning a special outing or playdate together.

Why can't I have those sneakers? Everybody else has them.

What do you like about them?

Will you wear them a lot?

How long will they last?

How much do they cost?

If you don't have them, how will you feel?

You can't have them because I don't think they're worth the money.

You can't have them because we can't afford them right now.

If you want to buy them out of your allowance, you're welcome to. When a child requests expensive brand-name items, some parents offer to pay the amount they would for an ordinary pair and invite the child to cover the difference out of allowance money or part-time earnings.

How much money do you make?
Enough to pay for most of the things we need.

Well, that's complicated. I get a certain amount of money from my job, and then I have to pay some of that to the government in taxes. The amount I get from my company is my salary or gross income. The amount after I pay the taxes is my net income or take-home pay. If you wish, give a rounded-off dollar amount. Tell your child this is family information you do not want her to share with others. (Don't count on confidentiality with a child under ten.) Then sit down together and go over basic expenses—home, transportation, utilities, clothing, and food—to put the numbers in context.

This question may be a sign your child is ready to take a more active role in household financial matters. Help him participate in budgeting by planning a family meeting to get everybody's ideas on ways to save money—more home-cooked meals instead of take-out, with everybody helping, for example.

Who earns more, you or Dad?
Dad earns more on his job because he's worked there longer and the kind of work he does pays better than mine. Also, most women earn less than most men. But that's getting better and I hope it won't be true when you're a grown-up.

or

Mom earns more at her job. I'm proud of her.
Your Dad [or Mom] and I both work to support this family.

Not all our work is paid. Doing laundry, driving children to activities, and cooking are jobs that we don't get paid for. We both contribute in different ways to our household, and we share our money because we are a family.

Are we rich? I wish we were rich, don't you?

Rich is a word that can mean many things. Compared to most people in the world, people in the United States are rich. There is a small number of very wealthy people in different countries who have many houses and servants and expensive cars, and they are much more economically rich than we are.

But for me, to be rich isn't just about money. Life with our family and friends is very rich for me. I hope it is for you, too.

Adolescence. One of the many ways the adolescent explores her identity in the adult world is through her changing relationship to money. With a summer job, part-time work, or baby-sitting, she has both new responsibility and the opportunity to manage some real money for the first time. Having money means power and status, and it looms large in the adolescent's view of life and peer relationships.

The typically self-absorbed adolescent often seems utterly unaware of how expensive everything is. She uses endless gallons of hot water in the shower, and astonishing amounts of shampoo. Having the "right" clothes is likely to be extremely important in her social life. For the most part, this is not a time to expect your child to be a pioneer in voluntary simplicity. Preoccupied with finding her place in the world, she is not very receptive to listening to parents' homilies about money.

But don't be fooled by her carefree demeanor. She is acutely aware of the high college tuition costs you will soon be facing, and of the reality that before long she will be making decisions about a career. She may be grateful to hear you point out that it's possible to look nice even without the latest outfit, and to have friends even if she doesn't own the most expensive electronic equipment. The more you can boost her self-esteem—with low-key remarks like, "I like that shade of blue on you," or "Your slam-dunk is a real winner," and with encouragement to participate in sports, music, drama, and other activities that give her a sense of accomplishment—the less she will need to try to do so by buying a designer outfit or $150 sneakers.

In order to believe she is capable of making good money decisions in the future, she needs to know now that we respect her choices in other areas—her loud music, for example, or her strange clothing. It is *not* helpful for parents to try to be "modern" and actually *approve* of her tastes (or, heaven forbid, imitate them), but if you need to object to something, try to state your reasons calmly and factually and avoid sarcasm. Even if she spends money on the latest fad, affirm her ability to earn money for the things she considers important.

Because she is increasingly interested in the workings of the world and her place in it, the adolescent's questions about money are likely to extend to economics. Encourage her to read the business pages of your daily paper or weekly news magazine. Invite her to go to work with you, or encourage her to visit a friend or relative whose work she is interested in. If she has a part-time job, she may be ready to manage her own checking account.

What's inflation?

If you buy a bunch of oranges today, they might cost three dollars. Next year they might cost three dollars and ten cents.

If you buy a car this year, you might spend sixteen thousand dollars. Next year you might spend sixteen thousand two hundred dollars. Each year things cost a little more. We're not sure why this happens, except that people who sell things naturally want to get more money.

What's the national debt?

It's how much the government owes—to banks, insurance companies, and anybody who owns Treasury bonds and bills. All of us taxpayers have to pay taxes every year to pay the interest on the debt, which is four trillion dollars.

What's interest?

When you put money into a savings account, the bank pays you to keep your money there. That money is interest. While they have your money, they use it to make more money by lending it to other people.

When you borrow money from the bank to buy a car or pay for school, you have to pay back extra for the use of the money. That's interest, too.

What's investing?

Investing is buying something in hope it will go up in value (be worth more money). It might be a work of art, a building, a new product, gold, or another precious metal.

Other People's Money

"My daughter came home from school and told me one of her classmates just got a three-hundred-dollar camera," one Manhattan woman told me. "I said, 'Wow, that's overwhelming!' She agreed." Actually, the difference between what we buy and what other people buy doesn't *have* to be overwhelming. It depends on how you look at it. One of the greatest blessings we can offer our child is the opportunity to discover that she can have less than others and still be contented.

Children find it less difficult to deal with the fact that others have more when they feel supported and encouraged to pursue their own hobbies and interests. For example, if your child shows a real eagerness to learn photography, she doesn't need a three-hundred-dollar camera. Start her out with a simple one. If she stays with it, bring her to a photographic equipment store and invite her to choose a good secondhand camera with enough features and flexibility to take fine photographs. Eventually you might let her turn a closet into a darkroom. It's not the price tag on the camera that matters; it's the support you give to your child's enthusiasm.

When a child feels she has enough to meet her real needs, the fact that others spend lavishly can even seem downright *strange.* "We brought our kids up knowing you can buy almost anything at a discount," one man told me. "The other day my sixteen-year-old told me about a friend of his who had bought a new stereo. 'And he paid *full price,* Dad,' my son told me. 'Wasn't that stupid?' "

The cost of a thing is the amount of what I call life which is required to be exchanged for it, immediately or in the long run.

—Henry David Thoreau

Why is Tommy's family so rich?

Tommy's parents earn a lot of money in their jobs.

Tommy's family inherited money from their grandparents. Inheriting means getting money from someone after he or she dies.

Why are there poor people?

Many people who are poor work very hard but their jobs don't pay enough to buy the things they need, like food, housing, and health care. Other poor people don't have a job at all for a long time—because they don't have the education or training they need, or because there isn't much work where they live, or because they don't want to get a job, or because they have lost hope.

Why do athletes and rock stars make so much money?

Every time an athlete plays on television, lots of people turn on the set to see him or her. The companies that advertise on these games know that they'll get a lot of people to see their commercials if they sponsor (pay for) the televising of these games. Then they have a better chance of getting people to buy their products, and they're willing to pay for that. Athletes don't usually play for a long time, though, so unless they learn to save and invest their money, they may not have much left after their playing career is over. Then they need to find other work.

Rock stars make a lot of money because they sell a lot of recordings. Also, every time a radio station plays one of their songs the rock star gets money.

Hard Times

"Christmas won't be Christmas without any presents," grumbled Jo, lying on the rug.

"It's so dreadful to be poor!" sighed Meg, looking down at her old dress.

"I don't think it's fair for some girls to have plenty of pretty things, and other girls nothing at all," added little Amy, with an injured sniff.

"We've got father and mother and each other," said Beth contentedly, from her corner.

—Louisa May Alcott, *Little Women*

Today's children know there's nothing picturesque or charming about poverty. They tend to perceive hard times in cataclysmic terms. When a parent loses a job, often the first question a child asks is "Are we going to be homeless?"

As for parents, answering is difficult because money problems are so painful. It's especially hard to have to tell a child that your economic setback will directly affect her life—that there will be no piano lessons for a while, no big presents at holiday time, or even that you will need to move in order to cut costs.

As with any topic you are anxious or angry about, think through what you want to say before talking with your child. If your child asks a question you are unprepared to answer calmly, say, "I'm glad you asked me that. I really want to give you a good answer. Let's plan to sit down after dinner so we can really talk." Now you have time to compose your response.

Be honest, but keep your discussion simple and reassuring. Instead of "There isn't going to be any Christmas this year," tell her, "We don't have as much money to spend on presents this year. Maybe you can think of something special I could make for you. And maybe you can help me bake cookies to give away. We'll have a wonderful holiday." In the long run, this is much more reassuring than running up credit-card bills in a guilt-ridden attempt to make your little ones believe that nothing has changed. With your love and support, going through a difficult time can be an opportunity for your child to discover that although money is important, it isn't everything.

That doesn't mean it's wise to put on a brave front and avoid sharing negative feelings altogether. If your child suspects that you are hiding something from her, she may well exaggerate the dangers. Instead, briefly acknowledge your concern, help your child put the money problem in perspective, and offer reassurance. "I'm upset that I lost my job, because I liked it," you might say. "I'm worried about how long it will take me to find a new one. But times are hard for a lot of people now. I'm good at what I do. We'll manage." Be sure to set aside time to share your feelings with friends or other caring adults so that you have the emotional resources to support your child.

Are we poor?
We don't have as much money as I wish we did. But we have enough for what we need.
Things are tight right now, but they'll be better soon.

Why doesn't Daddy pay his child support?
I don't know why. I wish he did.

Now that you've lost your job, are we going to be homeless?

No, we won't be homeless. Daddy and Mommy have been saving so that we would have money to use when times get hard. So we can live on our savings, severance pay from my company, and unemployment checks from the government. We will have a place to live, and you will see your friends, and sleep in your room, just as you've always done.

What will happen if you don't find another job?

I'm sad and angry I lost my job, and I worry about finding a new one, but I know that I will find another job. I have a good education, I've always been a hard worker, and I'm willing to learn new ideas and new ways of doing things.

Pocket Money

A child's allowance—given with no strings attached—is one way parents teach the importance of learning how to manage money. An allowance works best as a learning tool if it is big enough to provide for one hobby or treat each week, with some left over to save for special purchases—but not *so* big that she can afford big-ticket items beyond the level of comfort Mom and Dad are accustomed to. If your child is regularly asking for advances, she may need help learning to comparison-shop, or the time may be right to give her a raise.

Can I have an advance on my allowance?

I'd be happy to bring you back to this store next week when you have enough money to pay for the item you want.

or

Since we're only visiting this store today [on a trip or out-of-town visit] I'm willing to give you an advance.

Giving It Away

"Wealth is like muck," wrote Sir Francis Bacon. "It is not good but if it be spread." At school, in the congregation, and as part of other community functions, children have opportunities to participate in clothing or food drives and to raise money for good causes. But seeing parents and other respected adults giving regularly of their own time and money teaches a child to make giving an integral part of life.

When a telephone request for funds interrupts your dinner, why not use the opportunity to discuss the call with the whole family? Tell the caller to try again another night, or to send you a written request with additional information, because you would like to discuss the pledge decision with your family. Explain to your child that a pledge is a promise, in this case a promise to send money. Talk over the decision as a group. Some of the questions you might like to consider are

- How much money will we give away this year? You are more likely to make donations if you include charitable giving as a line-item on the household budget, along with utilities, clothing, and recreation.
- How will our money be used by this organization?
- Is this a worthy cause? Is it one that has special meaning for our family or community?
- How can we learn more about the organization? Find out if a newsletter or annual report is available.
- Does the organization provide opportunities to back up our financial contribution with other kinds of involve-

ment? Ask if you can correspond with or meet aid recipients, participate in work projects together, or lobby your Washington representatives. Are you likely to get involved with this issue?

- When did we last give to this organization? How much do we want to give now? Or why do we not want to give at this time?
- Is this a cause that relates to an issue our family feels committed to? No one can give to *every* organization. Giving means the most when you and your family get personally involved.

Exploring Together

Talk about the family finances. Let your children know that you save for emergencies. Show them a credit-card bill, and an investment dividend check.

- With young children, play show-and-tell. Lay out ten one-dollar bills on the kitchen table. Put four bills in one pile. "That's how much it costs us to run our home every month." Set aside two bills for food, one for clothing. Split the last one among entertainment, vacation, and savings.
- If your child is eight or nine, you can begin to talk about hidden costs—insurance, telephone, utilities. Mention the things you're saving for—a bigger home, college, a career change or a "rainy day."
- Instead of letting your child fill the supermarket cart with snacks and treats, teach her to comparison-shop.

By nine or ten, she can even learn to use the unit-pricing labels.

- Day by day, talk about the choices you make between time and money. Do you save by doing your own home or car repairs? Do you spend on take-out food or TV dinners so that you save the time to read aloud to your kids after work?

Let your child help with paperwork. Instead of looking gloomily at the pile of bills and receipts you need to sort through every month, offer your child a part-time job as your "assistant." You end up with a fun shared activity and give her experience in household finance at the same time. A nine-year-old can fill out checks for you to sign, stuff envelopes, and sort receipts into shoeboxes or files. Younger children can put return labels and stamps on envelopes. Pay by the hour, or offer a certain amount per piece of mail. Take your child to the bank to set up a savings account for her earnings.

Make time for the good things in life that really are free. Between birthday parties and trips to the mall, spend some quiet time in a natural setting. Take advantage of your child's interest in the environment to point out how conserving natural resources and wildlife habitats are also aspects of stewardship.

The Parent's Path

The better we know our own feelings and motives when it comes to money, the more effectively we can respond to our children's questions. These exercises can help you explore the role of money in your life, and how you feel about money, so that you can bring greater awareness of your own life experiences to discussions with your child.

Write your money autobiography. One way to explore what money means to you is to think very concretely about your experiences with it. Did you grow up in a family that was struggling, middle-class, or wealthy? What was your family income? How well off was your family compared to others in school or the community? Did your family experience any major losses of money when you were a child or adolescent?

Was money discussed in your home when you were a child? Did you grow up hearing about the Depression? Did your parents argue about money? Was either of your parents an overspender or a cheapskate?

Did you get an allowance? What was your parents' attitude toward your wants—hobbies, toys, movies? Were these provided for? If so, how?

Did you have an after-school job? What was your first job? Can you remember the day you received your first paycheck? How did you feel?

Your money picture. What are the financial issues in your life right now? Are you worried about major loss, are you struggling, are you on a reduced income, are you working on investments?

Do you have a savings account? How long could your family live on the amount of money you have set aside? How do you plan to pay for your child's education?

Your current attitudes toward money. Is your work satisfying, or are you doing it only for the money? Have you ever taken a lower-paying job because you believed it would be more fulfilling?

What are you willing to "blow" money on? When was the last time you bought something beyond your means? Do you have credit-card debts? How did you pay for your car? Do you have enough money? How do you decide how much is enough?

What was the last item you bought over $100? Over $1,000? If someone gave you $20,000 tomorrow, what would you do with it?

Love and money. Is it important to you to give your children the best of everything? How do you feel when you need to say no to a purchase? Do you buy gifts you can't afford? Do you try to protect your children from family money problems?

If you are married, what is the role of money in your relationship? When was the last time you and your spouse argued about money? What was the nature of the disagreement?

Have you ever made a purchase and concealed it from your spouse, or lied about the cost? Why? How would you have liked to justify the purchase? Would you consult your spouse if you wanted to buy an article of clothing? Go out to dinner with friends? Treat yourself to an expensive piece of sporting goods? Buy a car? One man was annoyed that his wife went out and bought a car while he was on a business trip. His wife reasoned that before their children were born she would have done so, and even though her work as an at-home mother earned no income, she wanted the same freedom.

Do you have friends who are considerably better off than you? Less affluent? How does the difference affect your relationship?

Books

FOR PARENTS:
Dominguez, Joe, and Vicki Robin. *Your Money or Your Life.* Viking, 1992.
Needleman, Jacob. *Money and the Meaning of Life.* Doubleday, 1991.
Schumacher, E. F. *Small Is Beautiful.* Harper and Row, 1973.

FOR CHILDREN AND PARENTS:
Barrett, Judi. *Cloudy with a Chance of Meatballs.* Atheneum, 1982.
Henry, O. *The Gift of the Magi.* Picture Book Studio, 1982.
Lasky, Kathryn. *Sugaring Time.* Aladdin, 1983.
Lasky, Kathryn. *The Weaver's Gift.* Warner, 1981.
Molarsky, Osmond. *Take It or Leave It.* Scholastic, 1980.
Viorst, Judith. *Alexander Who Used to Be Rich Last Sunday.* Aladdin, 1978.

· 8 ·

Death

A woman told me about the day when, at the age of five, she was told her mother had died. "Where is my mother?" she had asked a neighbor.

"She's in heaven with God," came the answer.

In our workshop session, this woman had taken a black crayon and drawn a heavy line across her sheet of paper. Above the line she put two stick figures. At the bottom of the page she drew another, smaller stick figure. "That's my mother at the top, with God," she said. "I'm the one on the bottom. From the time I was five I felt all alone, cut off from my mother and God."

I kept the woman's drawing as a reminder that our answers to children's questions about death may be barely grasped, but more deeply felt than words can tell. What parent wants to talk with a child about death? So much of a child's beauty is in the boundless energy that seems sure to live forever. Yet from their earliest days—with each experience of loss, big and small, from the fall of night outside the bedroom window to the passing of a loved one—children come to know something about death.

"Ashes, ashes, we all fall down!"

Some of the most popular games of early childhood began as playful attempts to cope with the reality of death. Hide-and-seek, for example, originally included chanting and music that suggest the game was about running away from death. The words "Abracadabra!" were supposed to magically prevent the plague. In contemporary Mexico on the Día de los Muertos, children eat candy skulls and buy paper skeletons and blow them apart with firecrackers. Today in our culture, kids still play cops and robbers shouting, "Bang, bang, you're dead."

And they ask questions. How long will the cut flowers on the kitchen table last? What happens when apples fall off a tree? Why did our pet die? "Mommy, what's a deathbed?" asked a seven-year-old after reading a fairy tale, uneasily eyeing her blankets and pillow. From weaning to the first day of kindergarten to going off to camp, children learn to cope with loss. And through their questions, they learn to go on, to find meaning in *this* world, to become who they really are in *this* life.

Why did my pet die?

Spot was very sick. When human beings get very sick, we put them in the hospital and doctors work for a long time to try to make them better. With pets, if we realize that they are not going to get better and they are in a lot of pain, the veterinarian gives them a special shot of a chemical that makes

them die. It doesn't hurt, and it's over quickly. Then the ani-
mal doesn't have to suffer anymore. We feel very sad, but we
know it is the best thing. It is against the law to do this with
people. If your family has a pet, it is advisable to be sure your
child is familiar with the concept of euthanasia long before
your pet's time comes. Avoid the term "putting to sleep."
You can use the phrase "put down." If a pet dies in an accident, tell the truth simply and express your sadness and
shock. *Spot was hit by a car. I can hardly believe it. He was*
such a playful dog. Don't say, "Cheer up, we'll get a new dog
real soon." Your child needs to mourn this loss, not get the
message that loved ones are interchangeable or easily re-
placed.

What happens to pets after they die?

When a pet dies, the whole family feels sad. We have had so
many happy times with Spot, and now he's gone. I think it's
important for us to have a special burial service to say good-
bye to him and remember some of the happy times we've spent
together. Maybe each of us can write a few sentences and read
them, or make up some special prayers.

Some people think animals have souls and go to heaven.
Others think only human beings do. But most people think
that the way animals are when they are alive—loving and
faithful and playful—tells us a lot about what it means to be
one of God's creatures.

All our lives, we are coming to terms with death and
dying. Although we often tend to think of development as
something that stops with adulthood, our understanding of
death gradually evolves. For this reason, answering questions about death demands a great deal of us. Unless we are

willing to wonder, and recognize our own fear, and shake a fist at the sky now and then, we cannot talk sensitively with our children about death.

One woman wondered what to tell her five-year-old about a family friend who had died of AIDS. Although this mother had no personal belief in an afterlife, she explained to her little girl that the dead man would be reincarnated. "I thought that would be a comforting idea," she told me later.

The morning after their talk, the woman discovered her daughter playing with her dolls and letting them drop one by one to the ground. "You're dead!" the little girl told them in a cheery voice. "But don't worry—soon you'll be alive again!"

In order to help a child, we need not only to try to speak on her level but to honestly draw answers from our own experiences, feelings, and beliefs.

Why did Grandpa die?
Grandpa was very, very sick—not with just a fever, a tummy ache, or a headache, like you or Dad or I get sometimes. Those are the sicknesses our bodies can fight. Grandpa's body was very old and very sick and he couldn't fight his very bad sickness anymore. Don't expect your child to accept a simple one-time explanation. He will continue to ask about the facts of the death (explain simply and honestly about the part of Grandpa's body that wasn't working) and wonder about other members of the family. By questioning he will begin to absorb the reality of the death. Don't be surprised if you are unable to offer a full explanation. As we go through life, we never find a real answer to the question, "Why?" Instead, we come to *accept* the reality that people die.

Why didn't the doctors and medicines make him better?
*The doctors tried their best, but sometimes a person's body
is too sick to be cured by medicine or an operation. Then they
die. I wish it had been different, but he was just too sick to get
well.*

Death and Development

Long before children know the word *death*, they are
learning to cope with absence, loss, and the idea of nonbe-
ing. Toddlers finish their cereal and announce, "All gone!"
They are willing to endlessly practice blowing out a match
and turning lights on and off, not to mention flushing
household items down the toilet. "Barbie's a girl, so she dies
last," observed one five-year-old as she let her Ken doll top-
ple to the floor. "Women live longer than men."

As the psychologist Robert Kastenbaum wrote in *The Psychology of Death,* "thoughts about death are intertwined
with the total pattern of personality development right from
the beginning, influencing and being influenced by all the
child's experiences."

Some of the most influential research about children's understanding of death was published in 1948 by the clinical
psychologist Maria Nagy, who found that children under five
years of age tended to think of death as a reversible process,
like sleep. A parent who goes out to the movies may seem, to
a young child, to have totally disappeared. A person who
dies, on the other hand, may "wake up" any moment. "At funerals you're not allowed to sing," one four-year-old explained to Nagy, "because otherwise the dead person
couldn't sleep peacefully." A child this age may try to make a
dead bird fly, or put a fallen leaf back on a tree.

When John F. Kennedy's son John returned on a visit to the White House after his father's death, writes Earl Grollman in *Talking About Death,* he asked, "When is my Daddy coming back?"

A young child's confusion is not surprising, because the difference between *dead* and *alive* is fuzzier than we tend to think. In his interesting study, *Philosophy and the Young Child,* Gareth B. Mathews struggles to answer five-year-old David, who is wondering whether an apple is alive. If not, the child asks, how is the apple different from the fruit when it's still on the tree? And what about an apple on the ground, which may eventually sprout seeds for a new tree? Mathews suggests that death occurs when the cycle is interrupted—say, when the sapling withers so that it will not grow into a tree or when the apple is brought indoors so that its seeds will not germinate. He also talks with six-year-old John who, shortly after the death of the family dog, reflects on the fact that he himself has arms, legs, and a head, and wonders, "Which part of me is really me?" The child, who knows that his toenails can get clipped or his hair cut, tries to figure out if there is any part of him that he can't lose without ceasing to exist.

Between five and nine, children begin to understand that death is permanent. Now death is often personified as a skeleton-man or monster (like the Grim Reaper), or as a kidnapper who steals away people during the night. Children at this age are less likely to express their fears about death. Instead they focus on trying to avoid it, like the "cooties." They can sound startlingly callous. One mother brought her six-year-old son to a party at a nursing home. The boy looked around and visibly shuddered. "We're the only people here not in wheelchairs, Mom," he said. "Let's get out of here."

If a person in the family or community dies, children at this age need reassurance: "Since Daddy has gray hair, is he going to die, too? When you get sick will you die, too?"

When are you and Daddy going to die?

Most people live to become old. Daddy and I are healthy and plan to take the best care of ourselves we can. Nobody can be sure how long they will live, but we plan to be around for a long time, to take good care of you and love you very much and see you become a grown-up. And as you grow up I hope you will learn more and more that not only Mommy and Daddy love you, but there are lots of people who care about you. Encourage your child to name relatives, friends, members of your congregation, neighbors.

Will you love me even when you're dead?

I'll always love you. Before you were born you grew inside me [or inside your Mom]. I counted all your fingers and toes when you were born. I love sharing books with you, watching you run and jump, and hugging you. I love watching you grow bigger and learning to do more and more things. I don't like everything you say or do, and I know sometimes you get angry at me, too, but I always love you. I'm looking forward to seeing you grow up into a big person, and my love will always be with you.

It is not until they are between six and nine years old that most children understand that they themselves will eventually die. Here is how an eight-year-old expressed this realization in Stuart Hample and Eric Marshall's *Children's Letters to God: The New Collection.*

Dear God, here's a poem
I Love you
Because you give
us what we need to live
But I wish you
would Tell me why
you made it so
we have to die.

Like adults, children often associate sickness and death with punishment. For this reason, in responding to questions about the illness or death of a child, it is important to emphasize that the causes are physical, not the result of misbehavior or bad thoughts.

Why did my friend die?
When a child dies, we all feel especially sad and surprised because children usually live to be grown-ups. Your friend died because he had a sickness [or accident] and there was no way to make him better. We don't know why a few children die and most, like you, live a long life. We wonder why it happened. We feel sad because her parents loved her very much. We will all miss her. Help your child slowly come to terms with this painful reality by making a "memory book" together. Collect pictures, artwork, and poems about his friend. Be alert for signs of anxiety. One mother told me her daughter said little about the death of a friend but, when her own brother went into the hospital for minor tests (with a clear explanation from parents) she "completely freaked out." Since chil-

dren do often get minor illnesses, a child who has lost a friend is likely to need reassurance that not every sickness is fatal.

Why did my brother [sister] die?

He [she] died of a bad sickness [accident].

We all miss him very much. Even though sometimes we feel so sad that it's hard to talk, if we can share our feelings and try to spend time together as a family we will all feel better.

You are healthy. There is nothing wrong with you. You do not have the sickness that made your brother die. Because a child is likely to feel very guilty about the death of a sibling, it is especially helpful to make a book or write an account of some of the memorable times you had together. In the course of working on the project, listen for suggestions that your child believes he somehow caused the death. Reassure him that no matter how angry he got about having to share special snacks or wanting to be first in the bathroom, he did not in any way cause his sibling's death. Tell him that you are still a family and still love each other very much.

Why am I sick?

You are sick because a part of your body is not working right. We don't know why. I know it's hard to hurt and to have all these tests. I know it's scary, and you are being very brave. I am here to be with you and listen to your worries and help you hold onto your sadness. Mommy and Daddy love you very much and we are making sure the doctors are doing all they can to help you get better and not hurt. As a parent, it is important to have support for yourself when a child is sick. Be sure you have someone to talk to, or join a support group.

Am I going to die?

The doctors are working very hard to help you get better. You are very brave and I know you want to get back home and go to school and see your friends. I hope you will be well enough to do that soon. I love you and I thank God for every minute we have together. I believe that when the time comes for any person to die, young or old, we're with God in an even closer way, and we keep on growing in love.

If I promise to be good all the time, will God make me better?

No one is good all the time. You are a precious child, just the way you are. We love you very much, when you're good and when you're not so good. So does God. We don't know why you have this sickness. We are very sad about it and hope you get better sometime soon. I think God feels the same way.

Healthy school-age children tend to repress the fear of death and get involved in community life—school, scouting, sports, congregation. They deal with fears indirectly, by telling ghost stories or watching horror movies. If a question about death does come up, be brief and reassuring. Try not to press the child with questions about his feelings.

Adolescents appreciate knowing that adults also wonder about the questions they are asking. They appreciate open-ended opportunities to express their feelings aloud, without pressure. Literature that deals with the theme of death can be a tremendous help. It reassures them that they are not alone in their feelings and helps them begin to come to terms with the reality of death (see page 199). Adolescents need to express feelings about death, and to find meaning that transcends it. "If there is a purpose in life at all, there must be a purpose in suffering and in dying," wrote the psychologist Gordon Allport. "But no man can tell another what this purpose is."

Grief in Children

Normal grief is a healing process. Through our pain and sadness and the disruption of our daily routine, we come to accept the loss of a loved one and to treasure his memory. In his famous studies at London's Tavistock Clinic, John Bowlby found that the child's natural grieving process has three phases: *disbelief,* with protests and insistence that the person will come back; *coming to terms* with the painful reality that the loved one is really gone (a stage when the child is likely to regress to more immature behavior); and finally *hope,* when the child gets back to his everyday routine and life goes on.

Infants, toddlers, and preschoolers may be cranky, unusually demanding, or clingy as they grieve. Their sleeping and eating patterns are often irregular. They may play out their feelings of loss by setting up pretend funerals or death scenes with toys and blocks. Because they lack a real understanding of death, they are often impatient: "Hasn't he been dead enough?"

School-age children may be shocked, fearful, and anxious about loved ones who are still alive. "Are you going to die, too?"

The adolescent is likely to feel strongly how unfair it is that people die, and yet to believe that it will never happen to him. Because he sees himself as invincible, a death in the adolescent's immediate circle of friends hits hard. He can begin to grapple with the philosophical reality of death through literature and by actively participating in commemorative activities—a memorial service, for example, or a scholarship fund.

In her pioneering research Maria Nagy found that the three questions children most frequently asked were: "What is death?" "What makes people die?" and "What happens to people when they die; where do they go?"

What is death? What's "dead" like?

Start with a biological explanation. *When a person dies, his or her body stops working. The person can't breathe, talk, walk, move, see, hear, or think. He can't eat or go to the bathroom. He doesn't feel heat or cold. He doesn't feel happy or sad. He can't see us or talk to us. We can't see him or talk to him. But we can remember him and everything that we loved about him.* If your child is young, be prepared to repeat this explanation as your child grapples with the reality and permanence of death. (At this age, they are used to fairy tales with happy endings. The death of the beloved spider in E. B. White's *Charlotte's Web*, whose babies live on after her, can help a child begin to understand the permanence of death and the legacy that each of us leaves behind.)

If your child is asking this question immediately after the death of a friend or relative, that is probably as much as you need to say for now. But if the question comes at a less stressful time, you can offer more information. With a school-age child, talk in terms of human bodily functions. *The person's lungs no longer take in air or expel carbon dioxide. The heart stops pumping blood around the body to feed the cells. The electrical impulses in the brain stop.*

What makes people die?

When people get very old, some parts of their bodies don't work very well anymore—their hearts, for instance. Then we say they die of old age.

Once in a while a very bad sickness kills a person. Usually when people get sick, they get better. But sometimes they get very weak, and their bodies can't fight the sickness anymore, the way yours and mine do. Then they get so sick that important parts of their body stop working and they die. (Avoid simply telling a child that a person died because he got sick; children and adults get sick all the time without mortal danger.)

Sometimes, if a person's body gets hurt very badly—like if he gets hit by a car—then parts of his body are damaged or broken. Doctors can often work to save people who have been hurt, but sometimes too many parts are not working and the person dies.

What happens to people after they die? Where do they go?

With a young child who is unaware of funeral arrangements, it is important to begin by answering this question concretely. (Avoid telling a child, "Uncle Pete is now in heaven," and explain that his body is now in the ground.)

First, there may be a wake. The family of the person who has died are visited by friends and relatives, either at home or in a funeral home. The dead person's body is in the room in the casket, either with the top open or closed. There may be many flowers in the room. It is a time to talk about the person and the death, and to remember the person as he or she was in life.

Then there is a memorial service or funeral in a church or synagogue. People thank God for the dead person's life. Some-

times there are speeches, called eulogies, when people remember happy times with the dead person and what they did while they were alive. The minister, priest, or rabbi will say something to comfort the dead person's family and friends.

Then the person's dead body is taken to a cemetery and buried in the ground in a place with a marker or stone with his name on it, so that people who love the person can come back and sit quietly there and think about him and pray. Bringing the body there happens during a ceremony called a funeral, when people who cared about the person get together to remember him and comfort the loved ones left behind. Sometimes instead of being buried, the person's body is cremated. That means it is put into a special kind of oven that is very hot and burned. The person can't feel anything because his body is dead. Then the ashes are put into a little vase called an urn and either kept at home or buried.

Try to be sure your child knows what a cemetery is *before* a loved one dies. If you are passing by in a car, explain briefly. You might want to stop and take a walk through one together, or show your child where relatives of a previous generation are buried.

Remind the child that a person's dead body has no feelings, that when it dies it does not breathe or feel or hear or see anything. (*Avoid* telling a child that dying is like falling asleep, or he is likely to become frightened at bedtime.) Listen carefully to your child's questions; one child wondered what happened to dead people's heads, since only their bodies were buried (he had learned in the bath that he washed his face, then neck, then body).

If the child is wondering about the immortality of the soul, begin by asking what he thinks. *What do you think happens to a person's soul after death?* Mention that you'd be glad to share some of your own thoughts on the subject. If you have a personal belief, share it in your own words. If you prefer to introduce your child to the concept that there are different ideas of the afterlife, keep it simple.

People all over the world believe different things about that question. Some think that's the end, it's all over.

Many believe that a soul keeps on living forever, long after the body dies. Some think it wanders around like a ghost. Hindus, who live in India, think a soul is reincarnated in a different body in a different time and place, and they think this happens again and again. Then when a soul is pure, it becomes part of God. Jewish people believe different things, but agree that the most important thing is how we live while we're alive. Christians believe that when we die our soul goes to heaven, which doesn't mean traveling to another place as though in an airplane, but having our whole selves be close to God in a different way than we are now.

Both Jews and Christians think that it's important to understand that our lives here on earth really count—how we live, and what we leave behind by helping other people and making a contribution to the world around us, are all important. We also live in this world through our children, through the people who remember us.

Earl Grollman, who is a rabbi, offers a helpful story to illustrate the idea that the soul outlives the body:

A little boy once found a bird's nest near his home which contained speckled eggs. Fascinated, he watched it for a long time until he had to take a trip to the city. Upon his return, he rushed to the nest to see the eggs. He was shocked to find that the beautiful eggs were broken. All he saw were empty shells. He wept before his father. "These beautiful eggs are spoiled and broken." "No, my son," answered his father, "they're not spoiled. All you see is the empty shell. The birds have escaped from the eggs, and soon they will be flying around in the sky. This is the way nature intended it to be. And so it is when we die. Our souls escape from our bodies . . . all that's left is the empty shell."

"But," asked the lad, "how do you know that we have a soul? You can't see it or touch it. How do you know?" The parent replied, "We don't have visible proof, but many people have faith that it is so. They believe that the soul is that part of God in us which lives on forever."

Perhaps the most important idea to emphasize is that our lives live on in the people who come after us. If your child is grieving a loss, this is what he needs to hear. Any metaphysical discussions that attempt to reassure the child that the person is alive in heaven are only cruel if you fail to acknowledge your child's pain and loss and connect with him emotionally. *Our sadness is a sign of love. Every time we cry for someone we have lost, that is a way of remembering them and feeling how much we miss them.*

Your child will be reassured to learn about the dead person's legacy to the community. Did he do social service work? Did he have a special hobby and share it with others? Do friends, coworkers, and other family members have memories to share? In *Death: The Final Stage of Growth*, Elisabeth Kubler-Ross recalled a ten-year-old schoolmate in her rural Swiss village who died of meningitis. "There was a feeling of solidarity, of common tragedy shared by a whole community," she remembered.

The way you inform your child about a death can help her grieve in a healthy way. Before you talk with your child, try to find time to share your own feelings with a friend. Then choose a familiar, comfortable place to talk with your child. Sit down and tell her what has happened. Speak clearly and simply. "I have some sad news to tell you. You know that Grandpa hasn't been doing very well for a long time now. Well, he died last night." If the death is sudden, express your own surprise. "Something very sad has happened, something nobody expected. Aunt Sarah was hit by a car yesterday. The doctors worked hard to save her, but they couldn't. She died." Be sure to mention that although you have some special things to do (make funeral arrangements, bake casseroles for the immediate family, etc.), you are going to be sure to set aside time for your child. Tell her you think it is very important to be able to talk about how she feels, and that if she thinks of questions to ask over the next few days you will try to answer them. (Watch for signs that your child is having an especially difficult time. If she is unusually quiet, unwilling to go out, frequently distracted, or preoccupied with frightening or morbid stories—or if she does not return to her regular routine after a few weeks—it may be wise to seek professional help.)

When you talk over a loss, gently encourage your child to express his feelings. "I bet you're missing Grandpa a lot now that he's gone," you might say. Then share a memory of your own. "I miss him. Right about now he'd have been setting out the tomato plants." Exposing your child to an overwhelming display of emotion can be upsetting, but seeing your sadness and tears lets her know she can express her own feelings. If a death is sudden or violent, be prepared for a great deal of anger.

Why did cousin Ann commit suicide?

I'm not sure. Sometimes people commit suicide because they are sick in their minds. They are so sad they think no one can help them feel better. They think the only way to stop feeling sad is to die. That is never true. Anytime we feel sad there are lots of ways to get help. There is always someone who will listen and care.

We all feel very sad that Ann committed suicide. She couldn't tell us how sad she was. We didn't see how she felt. We might feel angry that she chose the wrong way to solve her problems, but we love her and miss her very much.

What's "pulling the plug"?

Pulling the plug means turning off the machines that are keeping a person's body alive even though the person is basically dead. These machines have been keeping the person's breathing and heart going. When a person's body is not working anymore—the brain is not showing signs of life and the other organs are only going because of the machines—then sometimes family members, after talking it over with doctors and their minister or rabbi, decide that it is time to accept that the person is no longer really alive.

Why did Uncle Paul drink and drive?

I don't know. Some people think they can drive safely, even if they have been drinking. But nobody can do that, even if they are very big, or seem to be able to walk and talk just fine. They may look fine, but they are not able to see or make quick decisions in the way you need to when you drive a car.

Most of us feel angry at someone who makes such a terrible mistake. You might feel angry. I can understand that. We wish we could have stopped Uncle Paul from doing this. We miss him very much.

Did Grandpa die of cancer or heart disease because he was a smoker?

No. We don't know why some people get cancer or heart disease. It just happens.

or

The kind of sickness he had probably does come from smoking, although there are lots of types of cancer and heart disease that have nothing to do with smoking.

Today we know that smoking is very unhealthy. People who smoke do seem to be more likely to get cancer and heart disease than people who don't smoke. That's why Mom and Dad and your teachers try so hard to teach you that smoking is bad. But people didn't always know smoking was unhealthy. When I was growing up, lots of people smoked. And since smoking is an addiction, when you start smoking it's very, very hard to stop. I feel very sad that Grandpa got so sick.

Why did that person get murdered?

The person who killed him did a terrible thing. He wanted to rob him, and he had a gun. It makes me very angry to think that in our country it is so easy to get guns and be violent. It also makes me angry to know that there is a lot of violence on television that makes people think killing is part of normal life.

When things like this happen to someone we know, we get scared. We try especially hard to stay safe. We should always be careful to try to do that, but we also need to be able to live a normal life. Things like this don't happen very often. And the police are working to find the person who did this and put him in jail. If a child has witnessed the death of a classmate, teacher, friend, or family member, he may want to avoid the place where the death occurred. You may notice him reenacting it in fantasy play for a time. Without insisting or frightening him, take the opportunity to share your own concerns and feelings of loss and be sure he knows you are available to listen to his feelings.

Will I die the same way? Will you die the same way?

When another person dies, it reminds us that we will all die one day and we start to worry that the same thing is about to happen to us. This person died this way, but that doesn't mean we will. Most people live a long life and die when they are old. The important thing is to make the most of our lives while we are on earth. If your child is under six, it is important to clarify that death itself is not contagious. If a parent dies of an infectious disease, such as AIDS, keep your explanation brief and as reassuring as possible. *We don't know if you or I have the virus. In time we'll find out. It might take years. But for now we have each other, and we can make the most of our lives every day.*

Exploring Together

Make a book in memory of a person who has died. You and your child can include photographs, letters, drawings of special moments in the person's life, a list of favorite activities, foods, hobbies, and places. Keep the book in a place accessible to your child and plan to look through it together.

Encourage your child to participate in planning a memorial for a deceased loved one. Ask, "What do you think we should do so we will always remember Grandpa?" You might plant a tree in the backyard, donate some of Grandpa's favorite books to the public library, or start a scholarship fund.

The Parent's Path

How painful it is to talk about death—and especially the death of a loved one—with our children. We are much better equipped for the task if we ourselves have spent some time mulling over our own experiences with death and dying, and contemplating our own death. By doing so we become more aware of our feelings, more open to listening to our children, and more capable of coming to terms with death. Set aside twenty minutes to an hour for quiet reflection. Wear loose-fitting clothing, sit on the floor or find a comfortable chair, close your eyes, stretch, and breathe deeply until you begin to feel relaxed.

Think about experiences of death in your own life. Who died when you were a child? A playmate, a neighbor, a grandparent, a member of your immediate family? Can you remember how it was explained to you? Did the explanation make sense, or was it frustrating?

Think back to the most recent death among your family, friends, and acquaintances—a relative, friend, or co-worker. What was your first reaction on hearing the news? How did you observe the death—did you attend the funeral, send a card, deliver food to the bereaved? How often do you think about the deceased now? How was your life enriched by knowing this person? How was the world changed?

Start reading the obituaries. Maybe you're used to skipping this page of the newspaper, but each day you have the opportunity to read about the lives of a wide diversity of people—what they accomplished, who they left behind, how others remember them. In the process, death becomes a natural part of the narrative of life, and your own perspective on death will be enriched and enlarged. Although this is not an activity that ought to be shared with your child on a daily basis, do show him the accounts of people who have led exemplary lives, or faced extraordinary challenges and made a real contribution—people in the arts, government, science, or social service, for example.

Imagine you have one year left to live. What would you do? Travel? Try a new hobby? Keep your job? Do more community work? This exercise is an opportunity to understand how the awareness of death can give perspective and depth to our lives—and our children's—in the here-and-now.

Imagine you are eighty and lying on your deathbed. Look back on your life, not as it really has been, but as though you were a completely different person. Choose a fantasy. Perhaps you might have been a ballet dancer, a physician, an at-home mother. How would things have been different? What might you have accomplished in the world? How would you feel about it? Now, at the imaginary age of eighty, look back on your own life as it really has been. What do you feel good about? What were the challenges you faced? What are you leaving behind? This exercise, adapted from the work of Viktor Frankl, helps you find the meaning in your own life.

Write your own obituary. What did you accomplish in your life? What were your intellectual and artistic interests? Contributions to the community? Who are your survivors? What will they say about you? You might wish to try writing the engraving on your tombstone, or choosing the readings and music for your own funeral. In all of these ways, we begin to focus on that which is truly central, and the way that in the midst of the compromises and losses we all experience, our lives have meaning.

Write your own autobiography. How have you come to lead your life? Begin with your parents' life stories: where were they born? How did they meet? When and where did they have you? Include your school days, memorable moments (wonderful, sad, or embarrassing), career beginnings, marriage, childbirth, and so on. What do you know about yourself now that you did not know at the age of nineteen? What might others learn from your experience?

Dedicate the autobiography to your children and save it for a special day.

Books

FOR PARENTS:

Becker, Ernest. *The Denial of Death.* Free Press, 1973.

Frankl, Viktor E. *Man's Search for Meaning.* Washington Square Press, 1984.

Kubler-Ross, Elisabeth. *On Death and Dying.* Macmillan, 1969.

FOR CHILDREN AND PARENTS:

Grollman, Earl A. *Talking About Death: A Dialogue Between Parent and Child.* Beacon Press, 1976.

Krementz, Jill. *How It Feels When a Parent Dies.* Knopf, 1988.

Paterson, Katherine. *Bridge to Terabithia.* Crowell, 1977.

Viorst, Judith. *The Tenth Good Thing About Barney.* Aladdin, 1971.

White, E. B. *Charlotte's Web.* Harper and Row, 1952.

· 9 ·

God
and the
Cosmos

When Dorothy Day, the reformer and founder of the Catholic Workers Movement, was a young girl, she wondered "why some people had so much and some people had so little, and . . . what *God* thought about such matters." The child asked the same question over and over, until her exasperated mother finally said she had no idea what God thought. "It was then that I'd ask Him myself in those prayers I'd say sometimes when I was in bed and wide awake," recalled Day in a conversation with Robert Coles. "I'd ask Him to tell us, to show us, what He thought, so we could do what He wanted us to do."

Day's memory of her young, inquisitive self is a comforting reminder to parents who worry about having answers to all our children's questions. We have the most to offer when we are fully present to our children—present with our *not* knowing, our doubts, even our frustration and anger with God. As we let go of our need to come up with the "right" answers, we leave room for a child to know God in his own way, through imagination and daily experience.

If we worry less about telling a child what to believe (and what not to believe) and instead recognize each question as a "teachable moment" and an opportunity for open-ended exploration, then our dialogues nurture religious literacy and spiritual growth.

Stages of Childhood Spirituality

Religious education, wrote the British pediatrician D. W. Winnicott in a 1963 essay, "does not work unless the infant or child has developed in himself or herself by natural developmental process the stuff that, when it is placed up in the sky, is given the name God." Just as children pass through different stages of emotional, physical, and cognitive development, their understanding of God and their spirituality both change as they grow. Our answers need to change, too. We need to choose words the child understands, but also help him grapple with new concepts as old ones are beginning to seem silly or scary or unsatisfying.

The *preschooler* is interested in how everything got here and who made it this way, and often this line of inquiry leads to talking about God. One small boy pointed to a tree and asked, "Who made this?"

"Well, God made it," answered his father.

Next the boy asked, "Who made tables?"

"Tables are made by people," the father answered. All through the day the boy wondered about the origins of one item after another—chairs, toys, food, appliances. "After a while, I was getting so fed up with the questions that I started snapping out one-word answers," recalled the father: "God! Man! God! Man!"

As we shall see, although this boy was asking a seemingly simple question, he was trying to grasp the concept of creation, the idea that things and creatures are somehow made, a concept that is especially fascinating to children around kindergarten age, as they grow more and more curious about the events that lead to pregnancy and birth. He is beginning to make connections. How does it all fit together? he wonders. Who started it?

His line of inquiry can be exhausting if you offer only theoretical answers. More often than not, the simplest responses lead into playful, spontaneous exchanges. Think of your replies as so many cotton balls, ribbons, buttons, and stickers your child is using to create a mental "collage" of the cosmos, with himself at the center of the picture.

"Every atom in your body is five billion years old," began one father in response to a six-year-old's question about how everything was made.

"Oh, *I* get it," she replied happily. "I was up there waiting to be discovered!"

Appeal to your child's imagination and enthusiasm for hands-on projects. "When you make something, like an art project or a picture," you might ask, "How do you feel about it? Isn't it special because you made it? Don't you want us to write your name on it and put it in a special place and take good care of it? Well, that's how God feels about the world."

To answer a preschooler's questions sensitively is to enter into her world, to recognize the images and stories that are beginning to populate it. When rain falls, God may be crying or peeing. Thunder and lightning are God's anger. According to the pioneering work of Ana Maria Rizzuto, by the age of six every child has developed an internal concept of God. If we nurture a child with stories, her inner representation of God will be a positive, rich one. If she has only media images and impressions drawn from overheard adult conversation ("Oh, God!" and "God damn it!"), then for her God may be someone to fear.

One winter's day I sat at the kitchen table with my daughter, who was then three years old. Outside big, round snowflakes were falling thickly. "Look, Mommy," she said. "The angels are shaking their pillows and the feathers are falling!" Fortunately, she didn't wait for a reply. "And look! God sent down a letter!" she added. "It's on the windowsill. What do you think it says?"

"I'm not sure," I stammered. "Why don't you open the envelope and read it?"

She opened the imaginary envelope and "read" aloud: "Dear People, I hope you are having a nice time down there. I love you. Love, God." In the fanciful way preschoolers do, she was expressing her basic trust and her sense of being cradled in the universe. She shared it with me when I managed to set aside my own concerns about what to say, and instead joined her in play.

What does God look like?

God doesn't have a face or body that we can see or touch, or a voice that we can hear. No one has ever seen God with their eyes. All through the centuries, people have known God by using their imaginations and looking for signs that God is alive in the world. Offer your child an opportunity to draw her own idea of what God looks like, or some pictures of God's presence among us. You might wish to share your own personal experiences of the sacred—in nature, in helping others, in music.

What's a soul?

A soul is your whole self. Sometimes people talk about a soul as though it were something separate from your body—attached, like a shadow—but really it's the wholeness of who you are. And it's connected with all other creatures and with God.

What's heaven?

Heaven is mostly a Christian idea about where people go after we die. It's not a place with clouds and harps and angels, although imagining it that way gives us a sense of how it must feel. It's a new way of being with God.

In the Bible, the kingdom of Heaven is right here on earth at the moments when God's goodness and love win out over pain and wrong in the world.

What's hell? Does God really punish bad people?

Graphic images of hell—found not only in some Christian teaching but also in Tibetan Buddhism—"grab" children because in their moral system it is hard to conceptualize a just God who does not punish wrongdoers. *I think that since God made us and loves us, God wants to help us live as whole people. I know you learned the Ten Commandments in Sunday school. Sometimes it sounds as though if you break any of them you'll end up going to hell, just like if you get in a fight at school you'll go to the principal's office. But even when we do bad things, God loves us. God gave us the commandments to help us, to show us the path to leading a whole, full life.*

When I think of hell, I think of the pain of living in a way completely different from the way we are meant to live. Hell is being cut off from truth, beauty, and spiritual love. We end up

that way by making wrong choices instead of acting the way
we know is right.

Does God know what I'm thinking or what I'll do?

God isn't listening in on an intercom. But when you're true
to yourself, when you pay attention to your own heart and
mind instead of automatically doing the same thing everybody
else does—like when you invite a child to join you on the play-
ground even though nobody else likes him—then you'll know
that God is right there with you. Many people say we find God
in our deepest self.

How will the world end?

Keep in mind that this theoretical-sounding question is
an emotional one. Your child may have overheard talk
about the nuclear threat or the environmental crisis, or be
struggling with the idea of death, and he is undoubtedly experiencing the basic human fear of annihilation. Offer an
accurate answer, but don't forget the reassurance that comes
from a hug. *In five billion years scientists believe that the sun*
will explode and the earth will be wiped out. We won't be alive
then, of course. Not even your great-grandchildren will be
alive. And by that time human beings may even be living on
other planets.

School-age children are interested in the world they can
see and touch, in facts that can be proved, and in narratives
that have a beginning, middle, and an end. Their understanding of belief, stories, and moral rules are often surprisingly literal. The school-age child's notions of spirituality
often sound surprisingly pedestrian to parents who yearn to
impart a more sophisticated, less rigid belief system than

the one they grew up with. For kids over six, God is no longer the mystical-sounding ethereal force the preschooler knew, but more likely a person, represented by a man on a cloud, or by Jesus, or Moses, or even Captain Planet.

Children, egocentric as they are, tend to hear the story of the universe in terms of their own existence. As we struggle to answer their fundamental questions about the nature of things, and as we grapple with terms like the "big bang," it is helpful to remember that their wondering is motivated not only by a need for information, but by awe and wonder, and by their need for meaning.

When we teach only the "hard facts," we mislead children about both science and spirit. Then the wonder is lost. "Scientists understand more and more about the world today," one boy told his mother, "and once they've explained everything we won't need to talk about God anymore." The boy had discovered the "God of the gaps," the deity that people all over the world, in the absence of scientific knowledge, have invoked as an explanation of natural phenomena. Today, even physicists and biologists are emphatic that the universe is as complex and mysterious as it ever was. Einstein described his own calculations as attempts to "know the mind of God." As we answer questions about the origins of life and the universe, we can remind our concrete school-age thinker that truth is more than a collection of hard facts.

Did God make the universe? Didn't God make everything?

Theologians (people who try to describe God) and scientists have studied the question you're asking for a long time. They both say the universe is growing and living creatures are born all the time. That's why we can think of God as the creator who keeps making things happen today—not as someone who just started everything off. Think about your own body. You were born on your birthday. But every single day your body makes new cells, your hair grows, your brain thinks, and your heart beats. Living means growing and changing, for our bodies and for the universe.

Both scientists and theologians keep discovering that there is a deep order to the universe. Two hundred years ago a theologian named William Paley tried to explain this in a way that people would remember. He said that if you found a stone on the ground, you might just think that it had been there forever. But if you found a watch on the ground, you would see how carefully it had been put together, and you would decide that somebody must have made it. Since the universe is so complicated and seems to fit together in very tricky ways—like a watch—many people believe that's a good reason to think it was made by God. Scientists explain how the universe began when they talk about the "big bang."

What's the "big bang"? How did the universe start?

A long time ago—between ten and twenty thousand million years ago—most scientists believe the universe was very small and incredibly compact. All the galaxies were at the same place instead of being spread all over, the way they are now. Everything was stuck together in one very heavy place.

The "big bang" is the name scientists give to the moment when that very small point got very hot and exploded. The point got much bigger very quickly. As it got bigger, it got colder, and some of the energy that came out condensed into tiny particles. Now the universe was filled with stuff scientists call "cosmic soup." The cosmic soup turned into more and more different kinds of matter and particles.

As the cosmic soup cooled down, the particles collected into two kinds of atoms, hydrogen and helium. We still think of these two as the building blocks of everything in the universe.

How did the world get made?

Scientists think that after the big bang, gravity made the atoms of hydrogen and helium swirl into whirlpools and pull together very tightly into clouds. The clouds were squeezed so tightly they began to burn, and they became the first stars.

Later, about five thousand million years ago, some very heavy stars called supernovas exploded into other stars and planets, including the ones of our solar system. Then about five billion years ago our sun started to burn, and the cloud of atoms around it condensed into nine hot balls that became planets.

The earth is one of those planets. As it started to cool down, a crust formed on the outside of it. That's the land we walk on. Even today, it's still hot inside.

As the earth was cooling down, the water vapor in the atmosphere started to condense into little droplets. That was the first rain. The rain lasted for years and years, and the rainwater collected into oceans and rivers and lakes.

Scientists used to think the earth was covered with one big land mass that broke up into continents. But now we know that the continents have been changing and moving all through the earth's history.

How did life begin?

We don't know exactly how it happened. But we do know that four billion years ago huge amounts of the elements needed for life—like carbon and oxygen—were on the earth. Somehow energy took all these atoms and turned them into the basic chemicals that make up living things (amino acids and nucleotide bases). Scientists don't know how it happened.

The amino acids and nucleotide bases sloshed around in the ocean. Some scientists think that as they washed up onto clay beaches they turned into complicated molecules that were close to living cells. These started to grow and split into other cells until the ocean was full of tiny groups of molecules.

Who were the first people?

The very first ancestors of human beings were the ape-men, who lived 2 million to 3 million years ago. Homo sapiens *(modern people) only go back 100,000 to 300,000 years. Right before* Homo sapiens *there was a species called* Homo erectus, *who lived in Africa, Asia, and Europe. These people walked on two legs and looked like us, except they had smaller skulls.*

Some anthropologists (scientists who study people) think the first Homo sapiens *sprang up in several different parts of the earth at the same time. Others think they lived first in Africa. And others think that every person living today can trace his mother's family all the way back to one woman, who lived in Africa 100,000 to 200,000 years ago. These people like to call her the "African Eve."*

Were Adam and Eve real? Why do we learn about Adam and Eve?

Rather than dismiss the story altogether, or insist on it as literal history, we can encourage children to understand its power as *myth*. This is an opportunity to help school-age children begin to think in a less linear way. We can help them grapple with the difference between fact and truth. We need to live (more than we're used to) with paradox and wonder. We can acknowledge that we are not able to know the truth of a sacred story in the *same* way that we can know whether it's raining, or whether a door is open or closed. But we can hear the truth in it. *The stories of Adam and Eve, and the garden of Eden, didn't really happen that way. But parents tell those stories to children because they remind us of some very important things about life. They tell us that the world and everything in it was good when it was created. They tell us God loves us. They tell us life is precious, and we are here to help one another and care for all of earth's creatures.*

Keep in mind that there are *two* creation stories in Genesis, written at different times and with different plots. The first story, chapters 1 to 11, is probably more recent. It was written in the sixth century B.C. and is different from the creation stories of other cultures in the Near East at that time (such as the Baal epic and the Babylonian story), which showed the world beginning in combat between the gods and matter. This story presents one God who rules and creates just by talking. It emphasizes the orderliness and diversity of creation.

The second story, found in chapters 12 to 50, is probably older. It is written like a folk tale and focuses on people. Man appears first, before the plants and animals, and woman is created after man. This is the earliest "family history" in the Bible.

As your child encounters these contradictions—between the garden of Eden and the scientific accounts, and between the two Genesis stories themselves—you can begin to help her *open* her mind. Help her recognize that reality can never be fully measured or physically described. Offer familiar examples of sacred things that cannot be seen or touched—

love, beauty, and hope. *People all over the world hand down creation stories that tell each generation about the important things in life and what human beings are supposed to do. Scientists can tell us many facts about how everything happened. Their facts and theories are exciting and useful. But they can't tell us why the universe began, or who or what got it going. Creation stories do help us understand why we are here. They help us imagine our place in the universe.*

For the most part the school-age child cannot draw abstract meaning out of the sacred stories he hears. Stories—from the family, from history, and from the Bible—mean much more to him now than philosophical discourse. He challenges us to find the divine presence in the midst of our everyday experience; for now, he is incapable of looking anywhere else. He gets excited about Moses leading the Israelites out of captivity, and he has a vivid, dramatic appreciation of the journey's challenges. But he does not learn from theoretical discussions of the story's meaning. His understanding grows through the use of *analogy*, not abstract definitions. He relates one concrete experience to another. To help him connect with the Exodus story, for example, read several different stories about people making difficult journeys—the Pilgrims, the pioneers, the slaves escaping on the underground railroad. Encourage him to keep a journal of his own travels on a camping trip, a visit to Grandma, or vacation.

Because your child takes things so literally at this age, he is easily limited by overexposure to dull religious instruction. Encourage him to freely express his own images and ideas about God and the sacred. The less he is told to draw a moral from the stories he hears, the more likely he is to connect them with his own experience and inner life.

"I wonder if we'll all walk around naked in heaven," mused one six-year-old.

"No," replied her eight-year-old brother in an authoritative tone. "I remember in Sunday School we read how people asked Jesus if a widow married her husband's brother and kept marrying all seven brothers after each one died, and never had any children, whose wife would she be in heaven? Jesus said in heaven people don't get married or have bodies like us. They're like angels." By the time he is an adolescent, this child will be ready for abstract ideas about heaven as a state of being rather than a geographical location. For now, the universe makes sense to him when he can see it in pictures as concrete as Michelangelo's paintings on the Sistine Chapel ceiling.

Listen carefully for evidence that your child's concrete way of doing theology seems to be unnecessarily puzzling or painful. Even at this age he notices contradictions between the things he learns in religious school and the way the world works. One Dallas mother talked about her daughter's fear when stories of infants kidnapped from their cribs at night filled the news. "She asked me, 'Does God watch over me all night?' " remembered the mother.

The mother told her little girl, "Mommy and Daddy watch over you all night and check on you while you're asleep." With these words she reassured her that, although bad things do happen, her parents would keep her safe. She had understood the *personal* meaning of her child's question about God.

Perhaps more than at any other age, this is a time when we need to recognize our child's limitations. "Did Passover *really* happen that way?" they ask. Or, "Is Easter a true story?" In their everyday lives, school-children are very clear about the difference between reality and fantasy. They know that a story about a child who goes to school on the bus is real; another about a flying school bus is fantasy. When they hear stories from our faith traditions that defy natural law, it is hard to understand or celebrate them.

Is there really a God?

"Some people think there is," one mother told her son. Later on she told me, "I didn't want to tell him the truth—that I don't think there's a God. What could I have said?"

Acknowledging our own doubts is an important step in talking honestly about God with our children. The next step—and an essential one if we are to nurture meaning and hope—is to be willing to approach spirituality creatively, to leave a door open. What are the sacred moments in your life? Where are the holy places? What is it you would like to teach your child about that seems to be conveyed in talking about God? Is it trust, love for others, reverence for the earth, a feeling of self-worth? Maybe these are the things you wish to talk about when your child asks about God.

When I was growing up people told me lot of things about God that didn't make much sense to me. To tell you the truth, now that I'm a grown-up I don't believe the things I learned about God when I was a child. God is a name people use to mean many different things. I'm not sure what the name means to me, but I'd like to think about it. Maybe we can do some exploring together.

or

It's hard for me to imagine God as a person in the clouds, but there are parts of life I think of as sacred. When I'm out in the woods, when I do something caring for another person, or when I think of what a miracle you are, those are some of my ways of knowing what is holy.

Your child may be asking this question because she is outgrowing a concept of God she developed at a younger age. Now is the time to help her grow. *We can never know everything about God, or describe God fully. Maybe you're wondering about this because the way you've been imagining God is beginning to seem babyish to you. Maybe it's time to try to understand God in different ways.*

"God said to Moses, "I AM WHO I AM."
—Exodus 3:14

Why should I pray when God never answers my prayers? Does God really talk to people, or hear me?

Children who experience loss—after a death or divorce, for example—often feel abandoned by God. One mother talked of her child's nightly prayer asking God to reunite her and her ex-husband. "Why bother to pray? God's not listening," her child told her bitterly after several months. All of us—adults and children alike—feel abandoned by God at one time or another. As we grieve, we need someone to share our sorrow, often with no words at all. "I'm working with two little girls whose mother died," a child psychotherapist told me in a workshop. "How can I let them know God is with them?" At such times words about God often sound hollow or cruel. Our own presence, though, means a great deal.

If your child has experienced a loss, let him know you understand his feelings. *When you ask God to bring Mommy and Daddy back together as a married couple, then it hurts to think that God doesn't make that happen. I'm sure you feel very angry at God, and worried. Sometimes people who get married just aren't meant to be together. They don't match, and even though God is powerful, God can't change that—any more than he could make your red mitten match your blue mitten, or fit together two pieces from different puzzles. But God loves you very much and hears you, even in your saddest, angriest times. Mom and Dad love you very much. And we each want to listen, or just to sit with you when you need company.*

When the time feels right, you may wish to help your child think about prayer in a fuller way. *There are different kinds of prayer. Sometimes we give thanks. Sometimes we ask for things. But if we think of prayer as only asking for things, then when we ask God for something and don't get it, it seems as though prayer is a waste of time.*

Maybe you can also think of prayer as a special way of being with God, a special time for yourself. It can be a chance to share your feelings with God, even anger and sadness. The Bible is full of people who felt very angry at God and weren't afraid to say so. You can even tell God that you don't know where God is and you're not sure God is listening to you.

Does God do miracles?

"Miracles," wrote Willa Cather, "rest not on voices or healing power coming from afar, but on our perceptions being made finer, so that for a moment our eyes can see and our ears can hear what is always around us." *Sometimes when we use the word miracle we mean something impossible that happens, like a statue coming to life, or a very sick person getting better without a doctor.*

But miracles are also the amazing things that happen every day. A baby is born. A tree grows. A cut heals. One person reaches out to another. You're a miracle. You and your child might enjoy naming some miracles that happened in your life this past week or month.

If God is so good, why is so much of the world bad? Why doesn't God stop bad things from happening?

People have been asking these questions for a very long time. We all ask them when something bad happens to us, or when we read about a disaster in the newspapers. Nobody has come up with a very good answer.

I think God loves us and wants the best for all of us, just the way Mommy and Daddy take care of you the best we can and want to help you grow up strong and healthy. Sometimes bad things happen—we can't stop you from falling off your bike sometimes, or getting teased on the playground. Then we feel sad, and want to help you get over bad times. I think that even though God doesn't stop all bad things from happening, God wants to comfort us and help us move on. Try to offer a simple illustration from your own experience. Can you think of a time when something bad happened—say, someone you know lost a job and ended up with a more fulfilling one? Be sure, though, to avoid implying that God deliberately causes pain in order to teach us a lesson the hard way.

Is the Bible true?

The Bible isn't really one book. It's a collection of writings from many different ages. There's history in it, telling about the things that happened to the Israelites and to Jesus' followers. Like all history books, these have the facts and also advice and ideas in them that people used to believe but don't believe anymore.

But the Bible is also literature. It's full of stories of how people tried to deal with the hardships of life, to know God, and to understand what it means to love. Since we can't see God with our eyes in the same way we can see a tree or a person, God is represented in other ways—as the sun, or a burning bush, or the wind.

Not all the details in the Bible are facts, *but the stories tell us a lot that is* true. *That's why people have been reading the Bible for thousands of years.* "If you look *at* a window," wrote Frederick Buechner in *Wishful Thinking,* "you see flyspecks, dust, the crack where Junior's Frisbee hit it. If you look *through* a window, you see the world beyond. Something like this is the difference between those who see the Bible as a Holy Bore and those who see it as the Word of God which speaks out of the depths of an almost unimaginable past into the depths of ourselves."

Who wrote the Bible? Did God write the Bible?

The Bible was written by many different people over a period of thousands of years. First parts of it were handed down by talking or singing, and later on they were written down and copied over and over again. When people say God wrote the Bible, they don't mean God sat down at a word processor and did it. They mean that the stories handed down were full of life and truth and wisdom, and that God must have filled the hearts of everyone who told them. Rabbi Harold Kushner calls the Bible "a love letter from God."

The adolescent is acutely aware that the grown-up world is actually much more challenging than he had ever suspected. It is more contradictory, too, especially when it comes to religion. The adolescent notices that in Bible stories the God of love doesn't seem to love the Israelites' *enemies.* He indignantly points out that your congregation, which proclaims justice for the poor, has a mostly middle-class membership. He asks passionately what it means that innocent children die. What does all this say about God?

And, probably more important in the adolescent's view, where do *I* fit in? Adolescents are increasingly self-conscious; they are concerned with the type of person they are, they have an inner life, a place to fantasize about their role in the world. They reflect on their own views a great deal, and imagine remaking the world according to their own plan.

An adolescent is looking for deeper meaning now, and for the sacred in the depths of himself. He needs to explore his own spiritual life. In the process of breaking away from Mom and Dad, he is likely to bring his questions about God to friends and adults other than parents. Often an adolescent's questions sound naive or accusatory. Often the lack of truth and justice in the world are blamed on the "hypocritical" adults around him.

It's not easy to listen to a teenager's barbs without ending up in an argument. Try to encourage your child to explore ways that he can *act* on the principles he cares so deeply about. If you notice a pattern of questions about racial and ethnic bias, for example, encourage your child to get involved in an anti-bias group at school, or to start one. Unless the adolescent feels he can make a real contribution to the community—and is encouraged to do so by parents and other adults—he is likely to turn cynical and even depressed.

If religion is so great, why are there so many religious wars?

Human beings have a hard time with differences. People fight because of differences in skin color, language, and politics. That's sad and wrong, but true.

A person's religion is something very close to the heart. It's connected with our feelings about our childhoods, our homes, the holidays we celebrate, what we think is right and wrong, even the food we eat. Religious differences seem to be especially hard for people to accept.

In many parts of the world people of different religions live very different lives. Sometimes one group treats another one badly, or one group is richer or more powerful than another. They are fighting not about religion, but about power and money.

All over the world people of different religious groups are also trying hard to work together, and to learn to get along.

When Family Members Disagree . . .

If your child has a close relationship with someone whose religious beliefs are very different from yours—a spouse, grandparent, in-law, ex-spouse, or friend—you face special challenges in answering sacred questions. Know that you and the other adult each have a special role to play in your child's life. If you are troubled by a relative's remarks—whether you think they are too pious, too conservative, scary, or flaky—direct criticism of that person is unlikely to be helpful.

If you are in an interfaith marriage, sit down privately with your spouse and negotiate an agreement about your child's religious upbringing. Work out the specifics: attendance at worship services (one, both, or alternating), religious education, holiday celebrations, and rites of passage. There is no "right" approach. Some families bring up their child in one tradition, others in both, others in an improvised combination. The key ingredients seem to be respecting your partner's beliefs and affiliation, and avoiding turning the decision into a power struggle.

All families cope with differences. Avoid making disparaging comments about your ex-husband the materialist or your mother-in-law the religious fanatic. If your child tells you that something he has heard frightens, upsets, or perplexes him, listen and acknowledge his feeling. "That's a scary idea," you can say. Or, "That *is* hard to understand." For the moment, don't counter with your own views.

Instead, focus on your own spiritual journey with your child. Many parents in my workshops trace the origins of their adult faith to a few very special times with a grandparent or other relative who talked little about piety or doctrine but simply connected in an authentic way—by doing a craft together, cooking, going for a walk. The intimacy that you share will mean a great deal.

In the years to come your child will need to reconcile in his own mind and heart all that he hears within the family circle and beyond it. He will appreciate your support and respect for his struggle.

Why do we go to church [synagogue]?

I like to make sure that I set aside time to think about what's really important in life. I give thanks for what I have, try to think honestly about the things I need to improve on, pray for people who need help, and remember others who have died.

I like to do these things in a group. I like being part of a community of people who share a tradition—books, music, prayers, holidays.

I bring you because I hope these things will be an important part of your life.

If your child is complaining about regular attendance at services, avoid making it sound like an obligation. Instead, try to share your own feelings about one or two aspects of church or synagogue life that mean a great deal to you personally. This is especially helpful if your child is complaining that the service is boring. *Sometimes I get pretty bored, too, especially when the sermon is dull. But the part I like are the hymns.*

Try building a bridge between family and congregation. Include a hymn or prayer of your child's choice as part of a home ritual at bedtime or dinner.

If your *adolescent* has outgrown Sunday school and yet does not feel comfortable in the adult congregation, speak to the clergy about the possibility of increasing youth involvement in adult activities—outreach, worship, even teaching small children. If you make no headway, sit down with your child and help him plan an "alternative" approach to his spiritual life that might include taking a meditation course for teens, joining another congregation's youth group, or volunteering with a community agency.

Why don't we go to church [synagogue]?

Tell your child the truth. Rather than deprecating regular churchgoers, briefly share *your* experience. Then point out your family's own shared spirituality. *In our family we like to go for nature walks, work out our disagreements peacefully, and help needy people in our community. These are some of the things other people do in a congregation.* If your child persists in asking this question, offer to take him or her to a service at a friend's house of worship, or to plan a simple gathering to share readings or silence with family or friends at home.

What happens to people who don't believe in God?

As always, it is a good idea to explore your child's motivation for asking this question. Maybe she is beginning to be doubtful about the concept of God in her own mind. Or she has heard someone—a relative, baby-sitter, or friend—say that there is no God. Or somewhere she has heard that unbelievers are condemned.

I don't like to divide people into groups of good guys and bad guys. Even though God is important in my life, and believing in God inspires many people to be loving and caring, plenty of people through history have used their belief in God as an excuse to do terrible things.

I know quite a few people who don't believe in God. Some people don't believe in God because they see so much pain in the world. Others don't because they learned about God in a silly way that doesn't make any sense to them. Some don't because their hearts are hard. But even though I do believe in God, I have my doubts sometimes. And I know that for many people who don't believe in God, life is still sacred and full of wonder.

Can I be Jewish [Christian, Muslim]?

People know God in many different ways. In our family we are introducing you to our tradition—our prayers, hymns, and holidays. The people in our congregation aren't perfect, and sometimes you'll need to work toward change. But we hope this tradition will be important to you when you grow up.

But one day you may find that another tradition means more to you. That's a big decision to make, but if you really believe it is right, that might be the right choice for you. I will always love you and respect your decision.

Was Jesus God?

Christians believe that Jesus was an ordinary flesh-and-blood person, just like you and me, and also that in the things he said and did he showed us the face of God in a way no other ordinary person has. Many Christians pray to Jesus because they find it easier to feel close to God when they can talk and listen to a person.

Many other people think of Jesus as a very holy person who talked about God in a special way and was filled with God's spirit.

Whether or not people believe that Jesus was God, they do believe that God is much bigger than we can fully know or imagine. Christians, Jews, and Muslims all agree about that.

Did the Jews kill Jesus?

I'm glad you asked that question. One of the most hurtful things that has ever been said is that the Jews killed Jesus. All through history it has been used as an excuse to treat Jewish people badly and even to kill them. The Bible says Jesus was killed by the Romans. He was crucified, and that was a death

sentence only Roman authorities could hand down. The Ro-
mans considered him a threat to Caesar. People from all differ-
ent groups wanted Jesus dead. Maybe the most important
thing to remember is that Jesus was Jewish. Most of his
friends—Peter, John, Mary Magdalene—were Jewish, too. The
story that "the Jews killed Jesus" has been officially banned by
the Roman Catholic church, and is not accepted by main-
stream Christians. But biased people have used it as an excuse
to blame Jews for the world's problems for thousands of years.

Exploring Together

Go for night walks. Plan on these occasionally or once a
month. Check the newspaper to find out what phase the
moon will be in, and which planets and constellations may
be visible. Keep your walks fun by noticing not only heavenly bodies but everything around you: insect sounds,
smells, owls hooting, how it feels to be out in the dark. Your
child may wish to keep a log of the family's observations.

Your own creation story. Go for a walk and find a big, old
oak tree. Collect acorns, and when you get home wrap one
of them in damp cotton fluff. Place it in a plastic sandwich
bag and when it sprouts, plant it in a pot. Plant the seedling
in the ground, and imagine the day when a child of the future will sit under the tree and read.

Plan a family service. Invite your children to make up or
choose prayers, poems, Bible verses, or other readings, or a
musical selection. Gather in an uncluttered, comfortable
room or a pleasant outdoor spot. Limit each child's contri-

bution to five minutes. Close by praying (together or by turns) or sitting in silence for a few minutes.

The Parent's Path

Sometimes the words we say about God are hollow-sounding, because they do not match up with our own inner concept of God and the sacred. Even though we may have *ideas* about God as loving, our feelings may be fearful, angry, or numb. One way to connect with our true spirituality is to recall childhood encounters with the sacred. Many adults find this easiest to do by setting aside half an hour to sit down on the floor with a large sheet of drawing paper and a box of crayons.

Draw a picture of God or the sacred from your childhood experience. To acknowledge those feelings, or rediscover a sacred childhood memory, is often a giant step forward on our spiritual path.

Think back to the days when you were four or five years old. How did you think about God then? What do you remember your parents or teachers telling you about God or heaven? For some people, this is a happy picture of Jesus or Moses, or a member of the clergy. For others it may be a forbidding castle, or a finger pointing at a frightened young "sinner." For others it may be a bearded old man on a cloud.

Draw a picture of a moment when you felt connected with God—or with the whole universe, or with others all around you. Maybe you were lying in a boat out under the stars, or curled up in a familiar warm spot under a tree or bush.

Maybe you were listening to music in church, or sitting at the seder table with the whole extended family. Try to think back to a time when you had a feeling of wholeness and peace that you cannot describe in words. Chances are it was an unplanned moment, one to which you may not have given much thought in years. If you can picture yourself in that spot now, try to remember what you saw, how everything smelled, the sounds you heard.

Books

FOR PARENTS:

Berry, Thomas. *The Dream of the Earth*. Sierra Club, 1988.

Boyer, Ernest, Jr. *Finding God at Home*. Harper and Row, 1984.

Coles, Robert. *The Spiritual Life of Children*. Houghton Mifflin, 1990.

Cornell, Joseph. *Sharing Nature with Children*. Dawn Publications, 1979.

Cowan, Paul, with Rachel Cowan. *Mixed Blessings: Overcoming the Stumbling Blocks in an Interfaith Marriage*. Penguin, 1987.

Fitzpatrick, Jean Grasso. *Something More: Nurturing Your Child's Spiritual Growth*. Penguin, 1991.

Kushner, Harold S. *When Children Ask About God*. Schocken, 1989.

Moore, Thomas. *Care of the Soul*. HarperCollins, 1992.

Nollman, Jim. *Spiritual Ecology*. Bantam, 1990.

Overbye, Dennis. *Lonely Hearts of the Cosmos*. HarperPerennial, 1991.

FOR CHILDREN AND PARENTS:

The Adventure Bible: The NIV Study Bible for Kids. Zondervan, 1989.

Boritzer, Etan. *What Is God?* Firefly, 1990.

Brunelli, Roberto. *The Macmillan Book of 366 Bible Stories*. Macmillan, 1988.

Christopher, John. *The Pool of Fire*. Macmillan, 1968.

Cooper, Susan. *The Dark Is Rising*. Collier, 1973.

The Crossroad Children's Bible. Crossroad, 1989.

Earthworks Group. *50 Simple Things Kids Can Do to Save the Earth*. Andrews and McMeel, 1990.

Farmer, Penelope. *Beginnings: Creation Myths of the World.* Atheneum, 1979.

Hill, Douglas. *The Caves of Klydor.* Atheneum, 1985.

Katz, Adrienne. *Naturewatch.* Addison-Wesley, 1986.

L'Engle, Madeleine. *Ladder of Angels.* HarperCollins, 1988.

Lindberg, Reeve. *The Midnight Farm.* Dial Books for Young Readers, 1978.

McCloskey, Robert. *One Morning in Maine.* Viking, 1952.

The Picture Bible. Chariot Books, 1978.

Provensen, Alice and Martin. *The Year at Maple Hill Farm.* Aladdin, 1978.

Sasso, Sandy Eisenberg. *God's Paintbrush.* Jewish Lights, 1992.

Segal, Lore, and Leonard Baskin. *The Book of Adam to Moses.* Schocken, 1987.

Seuss, Dr. *The Lorax.* Random House, 1971.

Slote, Alfred. *The Trouble on Janus.* J. B. Lippincott, 1985.

Epilogue: The Challenge

One day I decided to keep a twenty-four-hour record of the questions I heard from kids—my own, the neighbors', visiting playmates. I walked around with a notebook. Here are the questions I wrote down:

"What's humping?"

The answer to this first-grader's query, which came up after hearing a playground chant sung by big kids, was provided by her older brother. "It's sex," he said succinctly.

"Oh," she said, and changed the subject.

"Is it true ladies cut open their breasts and put Jell-O inside to look bigger?"

There were two adults and five boys at the table for this question. The adults looked uncomfortable. "Isn't it illegal now?" one of the adults asked the other.

"I don't think so," came the reply.

"Anyway, it's not Jell-O," they added in chorus.

The eight-year-old boy who had asked the question was undaunted. "It's true, they really *do*," he said, delighted to share his discovery with his friends at the table. They all whooped.

"If that guy in the paper tried to kill himself, aren't they going to send him to a mental hospital? He's crazy."

This was from a nine-year-old who had seen the morning headlines. I swallowed my Cheerios. "Well, sometimes people feel so bad that they think there's no hope. That must be how *he* felt," I said. "But that's never true. Even when we feel bad, we can always get help."

He stared. I realized my answer had missed the mark. For now, the joys of a boy's life—baseball cards, soccer games, the mysteries of girls—were so delicious in his mind that suicide necessarily equaled madness. And thank God for that.

"Is it true some girls throw up so they'll look prettier?"

Another question from a third-grader. "Sad, isn't it?" I answered simply.

He and his friends grimaced. "Gross!" they all yelled, then ran around the room pretending to vomit on one another.

"What are those silver things?"

In a gallery a seven-year-old girl pointed to a display of Russian icons, each one intricately cast in silver, with pictures of Saint Sebastian, Saint Nicholas, Mary and Jesus. "Those are icons," I began. "They're very ancient things from Russia that people use for praying—"

The child's eyes lit up. *"Icons?"* she repeated. "Like on the computer?"

Parents and children have always spoken different languages. All the well-meant answers in the world aren't going to change that. "Whatever the one generation may learn from the other, that which is genuinely human no generation learns from the foregoing. . . ." wrote the Danish philosopher Soren Kierkegaard in *Fear and Trembling.* "Thus no generation has learned from another to love, no generation begins at any other point than at the beginning, no generation has a shorter task assigned to it than had the previous generation." We can help our child grow in wisdom, but we cannot *give* her the wisdom of our own experience.

My "experiment" reminded me that kids need to explore their questions in their own way—with their feelings, with their whole bodies, with friends who get the joke. As parents, we need to recognize when it's time to back off.

Children help us do that, of course. From the earliest, messiest days of infancy, they teach us to set aside our own priorities. They keep us awake. They open us up to wonder.

And they remind us that few answers are ever completely satisfying, nor should they be. Through the years, as we encourage our children to lead an examined life, we are reminded that the world's pain is no stranger in the family circle. Questions about sexism, for example, hit home when your daughter asks if she's as pretty as Barbie, or when you imagine her throwing up in the bathroom to stay thin. I often think of the words Martin Luther King, Jr., wrote in his letter from the Birmingham city jail, explaining why he was not willing to wait for race relations to improve gradually. "When you suddenly find your tongue twisted and your speech stammering as you seek to explain to your six-year-old daughter why she can't go to the amusement park that has just been advertised on television," he wrote,

> and see tears welling up in her little eyes when she is told that Funtown is closed to colored children, and see the depressing clouds of inferiority begin to form in her little mental sky, and see her begin to distort her little personality by unconsciously developing a bitterness toward white people; when you have to concoct an answer for a five-year-old son asking in agonizing pathos: "Daddy, why do white people treat colored people so mean?". . . then you will understand why we find it difficult to wait.

That heartbreaking connection between the look on a child's face and the shape of the world around us often sparks a change in a parent's life. By now we've made a place for ourselves, found work, started a family. But our children's questions remind us that life's harsh realities—death, anger, injustice—are still with us, just like the homeless people we try to avoid on the sidewalk. Long after our children are grown and gone, we will be left wondering. As we labor to weave our answers into the fabric of our days, we will discover that we are making our own lives count.

Resources

To sponsor a child:
Save the Children
54 Wilton Road
Westport, CT 06880
(800) 243-5075

**For publications
about children
around the globe:**
Oxfam America
Educational Resources
115 Broadway
Boston, MA 02116
(800) 225-5800

For books and recordings:
Chinaberry Book Service
2780 Via Orange Way, Suite B
Spring Valley, CA 92078

For recordings:
Music for Little People
Box 1460
Redway, CA 95560
(800) 346-4445

For books and nature toys:
The Nature Company
P.O. Box 2310
Berkeley, CA 94702
(800) 227-1114

For conflict resolution ideas:
Children's Creative Response to
Conflict
Fellowship of Reconciliation
Box 271
Nyack, NY 10960

Many thanks to all of you who have written to share your children's challenging questions and your own thoughts and experiences. If you'd like to write to me, find out about

workshops for your group or congregation, or receive a
copy of my newsletter, please write:

Generation to Generation
A Network for Families' Spiritual Nurture
P.O. Box 146
Millwood, NY 10546